First published in the UK by V&A Publications, 2007
V&A Publications
Victoria and Albert Museum
South Kensington
London SW7 2RL

Originally published in Australia by the Victorian Arts Centre Trust
100 St Kilda Road, Melbourne, Australia, 3004
www.theartscentre.net.au

© 2005 Victorian Arts Centre Trust, KDB Pty Ltd,
Darenote Ltd and various other contributors
Cover image © Darenote Ltd 2004

The moral right of the authors has been asserted.

Hardback edition
ISBN-13 978 1 85177 513 2
10 9 8 7 6 5 4 3 2 1
2011 2010 2009 2008 2007

Paperback edition
ISBN-13 978 1 85177 512 5
10 9 8 7 6 5 4 3 2 1
2011 2010 2009 2008 2007

A catalogue record for this book is available from the British Library.

Every effort has been made to trace and acknowledge copyright of the
images included in this book. Any omissions are entirely unintentional,
and the details should be addressed to V&A Publications.

Authors: William Baker, Janine Barrand, Kylie Minogue and Frank Strachan

Catalogue design: Erika Budiman
Costume photography: Jeremy Dillon and Narelle Wilson
Editor: Margaret Trudgeon
Graphic Design Consultant: Tony Hung

Type: Futura BT

Printed in China

V&A Publications
Victoria and Albert Museum
South Kensington
London SW7 2RL
www.vam.ac.uk

Kylie – The Exhibition

the Arts Centre, Melbourne
15 January – 25 April 2005

National Portrait Gallery, Canberra
13 May – 14 August 2005

Queensland Performing Arts Centre, Brisbane
6 September – 4 December 2005

Powerhouse Museum, Sydney
26 December 2005 – 7 May 2006

Victoria and Albert Museum, London
8 February 2007 – 10 June 2007

Manchester Art Gallery
30 June 2007 – 2 September 2007

Kelvingrove Art Gallery and Museum, Glasgow
21 September 2007 – 13 January 2008

KYLIE

V&A Publications

in association with

MELBOURNE, AUSTRALIA

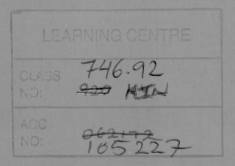

Front cover
'The Museum Dress', 2004
Silk screen-printed dress with fitted bodice and random fabric
swatches and trim. Pink and black tulle underskirt
Designed by Kylie Minogue, Frank Strachan [UK], and Lisa King [UK]
Realised by Edward Meadham [UK]

End papers/frontice page
Intimate and Live tour [Australia and London], 1998
['Dancing Queen']
Pink ostrich feather and diamanté 'showgirl' tiara [detail]
Designed and realised by Philip Rhodes [Australia]

This page
'Spinning Around' video from the album *Light Years*, 2000
Gold lamé hotpants ruched at sides [detail]
Vintage

Contents
KylieFever2002 tour
[United Kingdom, Europe and Australia]
Act One 'Silvanemesis'. Planet Earth.
The Distant Future.
Crystal mesh mini skirt [detail]
Designed by Dolce & Gabbana [Italy]

Forewords
Kylie Showgirl: The Greatest Hits Tour, 2005
[United Kingdom and Europe]
[Act One Showgirl. A Deco Review.]
Blue satin corset with sprays of star-shaped Swarovski crystals
and sequins [detail]
Designed by John Galliano [UK]

Moulin Rouge! premiere, Odeon Cinema, Leicester Square,
London, 3 September 2001
Black net dress with black sequins and antique
flesh-coloured lace panels [detail]
Designed by Collette Dinnigan [Australia]

Preface
Kylie Showgirl: The Greatest Hits Tour, 2005
Photo shoot, London, 2004
'The Museum Dress' pictured in bottom left-hand corner

Introduction
Intimate and Live tour
[Australia and London], 1998
['Dancing Queen']
Pink, silver and white sequin, bugle bead and fringe 'showgirl' corset [detail]
Designed by Kylie Minogue and William Baker [UK]
Realised by Suzanna Burgess [UK]

Collecting Kylie
On a Night Like This tour [United Kingdom, Europe and Australia], 2000
[Final Encore: 'Spinning Around']
White denim and Swarovski crystal hotpants
worn with jewelled leather belt [detail]
Designed by Julien Macdonald [UK]

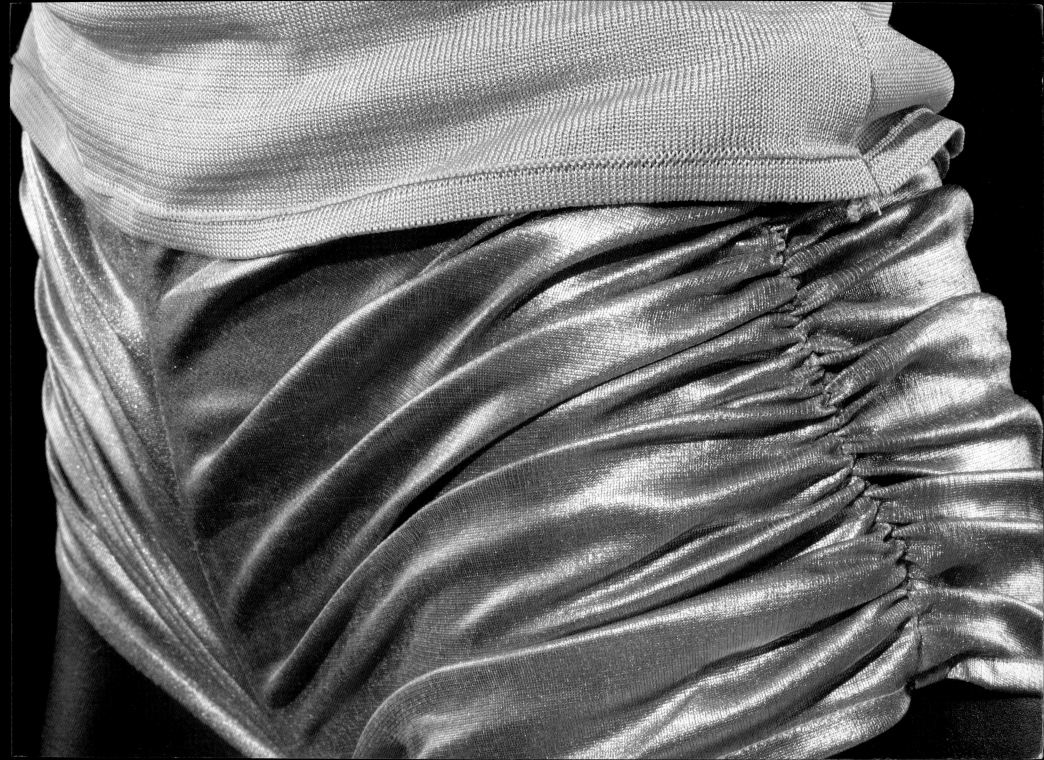

CONTENTS

FOREWORD
by Barry Humphries

I am delighted that Kylie Minogue has made such a generous donation to the Arts Centre's Performing Arts Collection. She is, after all, the natural successor to Dame Nellie Melba and Dame Edna Everage, and in a less egalitarian age she would be a dame herself. Her personal style is sexy and insouciant, and her costumes in many modes have always been an essential part of her act.

I have never worked with her in the theatre, but Sir Les Paterson has on one memorable occasion. It was a few years ago at The Royal Festival Hall, London, in an evening sponsored by The Crooner Nick Cave, when she sang one of Mr Cave's more sombre duets with the ribald Australian diplomat. All went well until the conclusion of the song when Sir Les found the proximity of the provocative chanteuse so exciting that he pursued her offstage wielding what could only be described as an equivocal weapon.

Kylie Minogue's career continues to prosper and her gifts bring delight to the world and credit to her homeland. We thank her for this joyous bequest.

Barry Humphries
Patron
the Arts Centre's Performing Arts Collection,
Melbourne
London 2004

FOREWORD
by Baz Luhrmann

Kylie has been a pop cultural force through the '80s, the '90s and now. Her story has been extraordinary, her stardom defined by a unique quality.

I came to understand something of this quality when I first worked with her ten years ago. We were shooting a Marilyn Monroe-like spread for our signature edition of *Vogue Australia*. The set was on the 20th Century Fox back lot in Hollywood and we were lucky enough to be working with legendary photographer Bert Stern (who famously photographed Marilyn Monroe for the very last time before her tragic death). We had been shooting for most of the day when suddenly Bert stopped and, leaning in close to me grunted in his smoky voice, "I'm not just saying this, the thing between her and the camera ... it's just like Marilyn ... hard to define ... She lets us in, yet she reflects light."

What he meant then, and what I know to be true of Kylie, is that whether she is acting, singing or dancing, apart from her innate talent and her professionalism, she manifests this rare quality, this warm-hearted, yet dazzling sensuous glamour. She lets us in, yet she reflects light.

Baz Luhrmann
Sydney 2005

PREFACE

By Kylie Minogue

Each and every item in this collection evokes a myriad of memories and marks a time and place in my life. It is far more than just a collection of clothes; far more than a collection of costumes. I am honoured that this part of my career has been recognised and is the subject of a retrospective exhibition.

Bringing everything together for the Australian exhibition was a wonderful, enlightening experience, as it allowed me to step back and appreciate the hundreds of different costumes as a collection, a whole. It afforded me a rare opportunity to reminisce and celebrate. Now the collection is going to travel to the Victoria and Albert Museum, the most prestigious museum of art and design in the world, and then on to the Manchester Art Gallery and Kelvingrove Art Gallery and Museum in Glasgow. All this is happening just as I'm about to embark on my latest tour of the UK. I am so happy to be able to finally share the collection with my UK fans.

Finding the costumes was akin to a treasure hunt on some days and acquired an excitement all of its own as I unearthed pieces that hadn't seen the light of day for many years. Though there are some items whose whereabouts remain a mystery at this point in time, I am delighted that the pieces that are here, from cobbled together to couture, represent some of the highlights of my career. Some have played leading roles in my live performances and videos, while others have been mere walk-ons, but each one has played its part. I have laughed and cried celebrated and waited in these outfits ... I will leave it up to you to imagine which.

There are so many elements that go into each individual costume, whether it be for stage, performance, everyday wear or video – camera angles, movement, environment, temperature, durability, where to put the microphone pack, what the dancers are wearing, the set design, the video treatment, the ease of putting it on and getting it off in an impossibly short time – all these factors have to be considered. However, the most important factors are intuitive and emotional: how I feel in it, and consequently how it affects my performance. The rest lies in the hands of my audience: will they love it, will they hate it? Will it be remembered or forgotten?

Some find their own unique fame and become icons in their own right, capturing a place in people's memories and reminding them of a particular song or moment. I never imagined I would have some of the world's foremost designers making costumes for me. I never imagined what impact a 50p pair of hotpants would have and I never imagined that a museum in my home town would be housing the contents of my wardrobe.

Most of my performance outfits are not made with any consideration as to how and if they will be remembered, but to suit a specific and usually urgent situation. The best outfits have often been the result of improvisation, and the unsung heroes of the photo shoot are more often than not safety pins and bulldog clips, helping a model size 10 masquerade as a Minogue size 6. The saviours of the stage outfits are industrial zips, quick hooks and Velcro.

Each piece in the collection has its own story to tell. The journey of a costume is often long and involved. The cumulative amount of time, talent and creative energy that has gone into this collection as a whole is staggering. I thank the many people who have been part of this journey. In particular, I would like to thank Katerina Jebb, Nicole Bonython and my creative director for the past decade, William Baker.

I would also like to thank my fans who have encouraged me to express myself and to take risks, and who have embraced even my less than stellar moments and fashion faux pas.

Were it not for my parents I'm sure this collection would be the size of a suitcase rather than an exhibition space. Thank you, Mum and Dad, for this and everything.

Kylie x

Kylie
London 2006

INTRODUCTION

by William Baker

When Kylie first decided to donate the contents of her stage wardrobe to the Arts Centre's Performing Arts Collection in Melbourne we all breathed a huge sigh of relief. Here, you will find her costumes presented on specially designed mannequins, each one basking in its own individual spotlight, preserved in its glory, loose threads and all, in defiance of the purpose and limited life span for which it was created.

Most of the costumes you see before you have been rescued from an unglamorous existence in storage vaults, cellars and wardrobes on opposite sides of the world. They have been liberated from a life of bin bags, mothballs and Fabreeze into a world where they are treated with the same reverence as a Rembrandt or a van Gogh.

At their moment of creation we could never have imagined a destiny further removed from the sanctuary of the museum. To be the subject of an exhibition that will be displayed at the Victoria and Albert Museum in London before touring the United Kingdom, is for us an incredible, if unbelievable accolade.

It seems fitting that the UK tour of *Kylie – The Exhibition* is taking place at this point in time, as it coincides with Kylie's return to the stage and a sellout tour – her seventh – very aptly titled *Kylie Showgirl: Homecoming*. It is an appropriate moment for celebration.

As Kylie's creative director and stylist, seeing the entire collection of costumes and accessories together like this is disorienting to say the least, and assembling this exhibition has not been an easy task. Looking backwards when the juggernaut is still steaming forwards is difficult to do, and this exhibition, like Kylie, will be a work in progress, constantly evolving.

Kylie's metamorphosis is not solely the credit of the stylists she has worked with over the years, as there is something very genuine about the way in which she dresses and presents herself to her audience. Before the various stylists and designers even begin to work their magic there stands an immaculately primed canvas. Kylie possesses a refined, almost old-fashioned sense of style that informs all of her most successful looks – she is simply chic. Her fashion sensibility is very Parisian, and in contrast to her contemporaries, quite old-school. She adheres to the fashion values and philosophies established by the glamour icons of Hollywood, both on and off-screen, and she has been blessed with a perfect diminutive frame. Stylists and designers love to dress her up because she is a pleasure to dress, managing to retain a strong sense of herself beneath whatever guise or trend she is experimenting with. Kylie more than just wears clothes, she interprets them.

Styling Kylie is an exercise in fantasy – of expressing the many different things that Kylie both represents and is. She is a gay icon, she is a showgirl, she is a sex symbol, she is loved by children, she is a business woman, she is a singer, a songwriter, an actress, she is a charity mascot. She is the girl next door. These are all realities for her, but the stage, the photographic image and video are all vehicles for escapism, where she can be all these things and more.

Designers are selected for what they represent themselves, and what their clothes can add to the Kylie mythos. Julien Macdonald's creations for the *On a Night Like This* tour shimmer under the weight of his trademark crystals and sexy glitz. Dolce & Gabbana's costumes are similarly glitzy, but possess a cinematic glamour. Both emphasise different aspects of Kylie. Chanel lends an almost formal Parisian chic; Helmut Lang and Nicolas Ghesquière from Balenciaga add an avant-garde body consciousness.

Visual themes and Kylie's styling flow organically from the music. The song inspires; it creates an ambience, an emotional reaction that offers different possibilities in the imagination. It is instinctive and intuitive. We try to define each song visually, with its own clear identity. From the street styling of 'Red Blooded Woman' and 'Love at First Sight' to the underplayed casual styling of 'Come into My World'; from the cheeky ghetto disco of 'Spinning Around' to the deco grandeur of 'Chocolate'; from the dynasty affluence of 'On a Night Like This' to the electro futurism of 'In Your Eyes' and 'Can't Get You Out of My Head', the styling evokes different worlds and fantasies, bringing the lyrics and beats of the song to life.

Kylie's outfits are not confined and therefore not defined by fashion. They have become symbols and icons themselves that exist today as a part of Kylie, a tiny expression of herself and her essence. The sequins, crystals and fringing that embellish the layers of silk chiffon and metres of draped jersey, exist as a glittering reminder of a modern-day fairytale of a girl from Melbourne who seduced the world; a girl who has grown up in front of all of us, a girl whose greatest achievement is not the record sales, the sellout tours, the business empire or the countless awards that she has earned, but the very human warmth and grace that unites her inextricably with her audience.

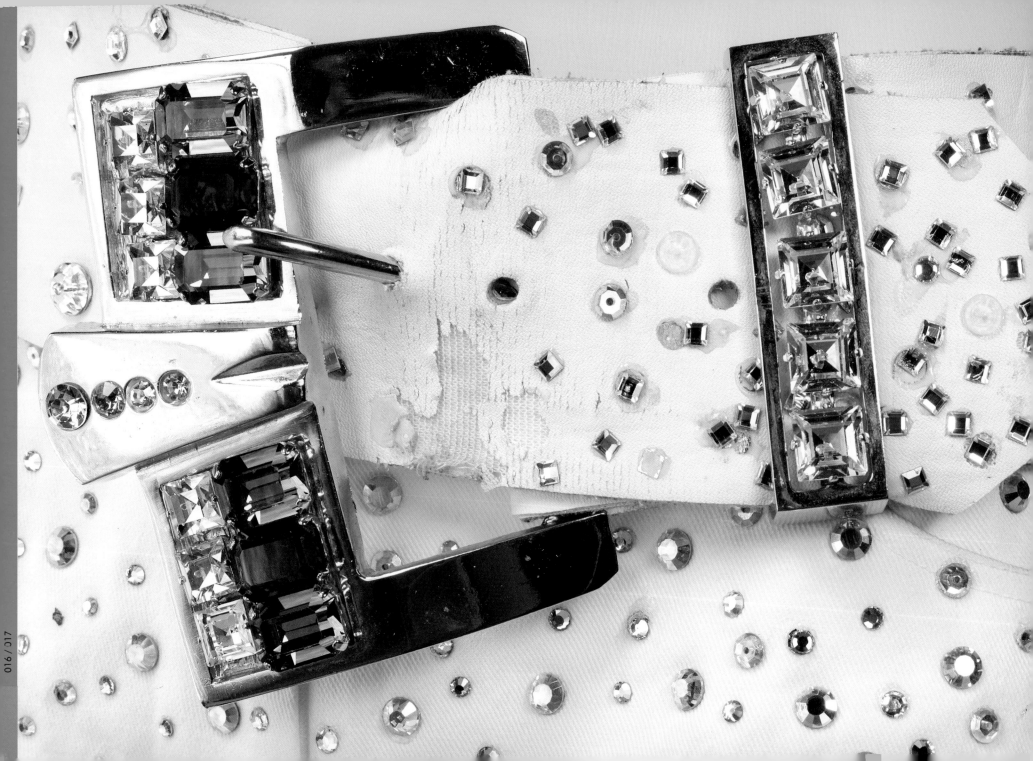

COLLECTING KYLIE

by Janine Barrand

The inspiration for *Kylie – The Exhibition* came from Kylie Minogue's decision to donate her costumes to the Arts Centre's Performing Arts Collection in Melbourne, a gift that is both generous and culturally significant.

Acquiring and cataloguing the Kylie Minogue Collection has been a remarkable and unique experience for all of us at the Arts Centre. We have been on an incredible journey of discovery which began in May 2003 when Ron Minogue first contacted the Victorian Arts Centre Trust with the happy news to the day the exhibition opened in Australia in January 2005.

This collection is one of the most significant to be acquired by any performing arts collection in Australia, being of great national and international importance. Kylie's wardrobe takes its place in Melbourne alongside those of Dame Nellie Melba and Dame Edna Everage.

So, what is collecting Kylie all about? To her many fans it means a chance to go behind the scenes and catch a glimpse of some of the costumes and techniques that go into creating the image of a mega pop star. For Kylie and her team, it has meant the preservation of costumes from many of the highlight moments along Kylie's road to stardom. Of course, like many performers who donate costumes, Kylie has been highly amused at the transition of the costumes from backstage into a world of white gloves, and strict preservation and display requirements. However, it has always been a matter of great importance to Kylie and her parents, Ron and Carol, that the more than 600 costumes and accessories are cared for appropriately.

The Kylie Minogue Collection comprehensively explores Kylie's evolution over the course of her stellar career and tells the story of some of the important transition points. Kylie's 1997

video 'Did It Again', in which four different incarnations are presented – 'Cute Kylie', 'Sex Kylie', 'Indie Kylie' and 'Dance Kylie' – encapsulates this well; however, today we would also add 'Iconic Kylie'. Her rise to iconic status can be seen through the collection from cute girl next door ('I Should Be So Lucky', 1989) to the sexy confidence of 'Better the Devil You Know' (1990) to the 'indie' deConstruction phase ('Confide in Me', 1994), to the looks behind 'Spinning Around' (2000) and 'Can't Get You Out of My Head', 2001. The tour costumes chart the development of 'Showgirl Kylie'.

Kylie's commitment to ensuring the collection is completely up to date has meant that costumes from her *Kylie Showgirl: The Greatest Hits Tour*, were received literally just in time for inclusion in the exhibition and this catalogue. Whenever Kylie performs we now know we will be contacted about the potential acquisition of her latest costumes.

Kylie has always had an interest in fashion design, which is reflected in the ways she collaborates creatively with major international and emerging designers and her continuing interest in vintage clothing. In her early years, Kylie worked with leading Australian designers such as Morrissey Edmiston, Ian McMaugh and Stephen Galloway, who are all represented in the collection. These links to Australia have been maintained throughout her career, and include Mark Burnett, who designed several costumes for Kylie's 1998 *Intimate and Live* tour.

Once she became a performer on the international stage it wasn't long before leading designers were knocking at her door. Those who succeeded were able to realise a sparkling array of interesting and cutting-edge looks. One of Kylie's hallmark collaborations has been with Dolce & Gabbana, who designed the complete wardrobe for her *KylieFever2002* tour. The entire sequence of eight costumes, in which Kylie metamorphosed from an intergalactic goddess to urban woman are now preserved in the collection.

The Kylie Minogue Collection encompasses all dimensions of Kylie's career as a major international artist of both the twentieth and twenty-first centuries. One of its unique characteristics is the almost seamless transition that has taken place between

her choice of costumes for her videos, tours and special performances and her appearances on the red carpet. These stylish, fashionable outfits are integral to the collection, and many of them represent Kylie's most important moments: we can follow her as she steps out in a Collette Dinnigan creation at the 2001 premiere of *Moulin Rouge!* or receives a Grammy Award in 2004, dazzling in a gown by Martine Sitbon.

From a distance it is easy to imagine that Kylie's costumes have an almost untouchable perfection, an illusion that is carried off with panache on stage and screen. It is an integral part of the mystique of performance. However, the acquisition has enabled us to get close to each costume and gain a clear understanding of the realities. Particularly among the tour costumes, you will find wear and tear and evidence of use – fabric abraded by microphone packs, and secret devices such as Velcro for a quick change.

When we began researching the collection and considering how best to present and explore Kylie's story as a contemporary performer, we decided to take a thematic approach. Music and video, tours, special performances, style (red carpet) and icon became the framework around which we decided what to include from such a large and important collection. We also decided on a sixth theme – image – to look at Kylie through the eyes of well-known international photographers.

Kylie – The Exhibition was greeted with acclaim by audiences all around Australia, attracting almost 500,000 visitors. The Arts Centre, Melbourne is delighted that the exhibition is now travelling to the UK where it will be seen at the Victoria and Albert Museum, Manchester Art Gallery, and Kelvingrove Art Gallery and Museum, Glasgow. The catalogue has been updated to include Kylie's stunning *Kylie Showgirl: The Greatest Hits Tour* costumes by John Galliano and Karl Lagerfeld [for Chanel Couture].

We thank Kylie and Carol and Ron Minogue for enabling exhibition visitors all around the world to enjoy and appreciate the Kylie Minogue Collection and for entrusting the Arts centre, Melbourne with such a wonderful gift.

THE MUSIC & VIDEOS

STOP PULL SHOT

ROLL 26   SCENE 51   TAKE 1

FPS 33Y   10.01.52.06

KYLIE "I BELIEVE IN YOU"

VERNIE YEUNG   JOB: BD70

SIMON CHAUDOIR   16-10-04

The promotional video or 'promo' has been an essential element in the promotion of pop records since the launch of MTV in the early 1980s.

A successful Kylie video is the result of collaborations between directors of photography, editors, the art department, lighting specialists, stylists, hair and make-up artists, and choreographers, brought to life by a director's vision and Kylie's interpretation and performance.

In most cases the chosen song is first sent out to several handpicked directors. Each director writes a visual proposal (called a treatment – their vision of how the video will look). After they have been reviewed, Kylie, her creative team and record company representatives all choose the director they feel is best suited to bring the song to life.

The treatment is then modified and adapted as required. The intended shots are storyboarded (each scene of the video is illustrated) and meticulously planned to help prepare for every eventuality. Hours are spent ensuring that all aspects of the video – location, lighting, dancers, set design and costumes – will work in harmony to create a finished product that is greater than the sum of its parts, and that will best complement the song.

Kylie enjoys experimenting with fashion in her music videos, and most of them depict her sporting several different looks. Videos allow outfits, hair and make-up to be more adventurous and risqué than in live performance, thanks to controlled lighting, special effects and the editing room. Kylie's videos have helped define her status as a pop star, creating her most iconic moments: the hot pink spacesuit, the white split jumpsuit and, of course, the burnished gold hotpants.

Kylie's videos have been shot in locations across the globe, including Paris, Rio, Los Angeles, Melbourne, London and Barcelona. The progression from the early days of 'I Should Be So Lucky' to the most recent 'Giving You Up' has been substantial. However, despite glamorous end results, little has changed behind the scenes. Videos are still the product of long days spent in freezing studios or sweltering in the midday sun, challenging choreography rehearsals, night-time shoots, water scenes and flying harness work. As Kylie once joked on set, "pain is fleeting, video is forever".

Watching the back catalogue of Kylie's videos reveals her staggering journey through the world of pop culture, fashion and creativity.

Previous page
'I Believe in You', London, 2004
Opposite
'Did It Again', London, 1998

IKEGAMI 14" MONITOR NO-1 12VOLT-240VOLT

POWER   P.L. TALLY   V.HOLD   H.HOLD   BRIGHT.   CONT.   NORM

OFF   ON   Ikegami   UNDER

INDIE KYL1E

CN 2Q567041103

'I Should Be So Lucky' [1987] video
from the album *Kylie*, 1988

Video directed by Chris Langman

White cotton muslin dress with over-sized
pocket detail
Designed by Jenny Bannister [Australia]

'Je Ne Sais Pas Pourquoi' video
from the album *Kylie*, 1988

Video directed by Chris Langman

Grey strapless rayon twill dress
with sweetheart neckline
Designer unknown

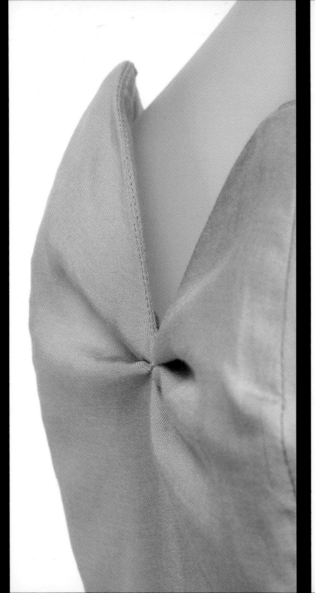

'Hand on Your Heart' video from
the album *Enjoy Yourself*, 1989

Video directed by Chris Langman

Yellow silk dress with halter neckline
and blue appliqué heart trim
Designer unknown

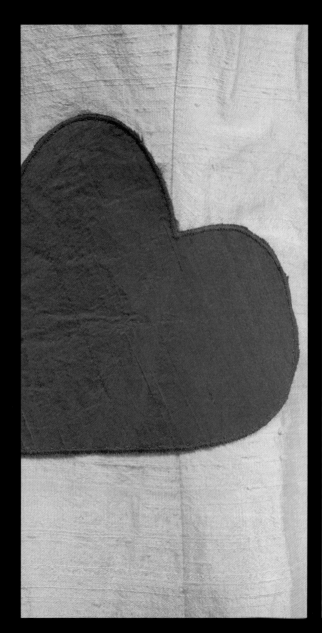

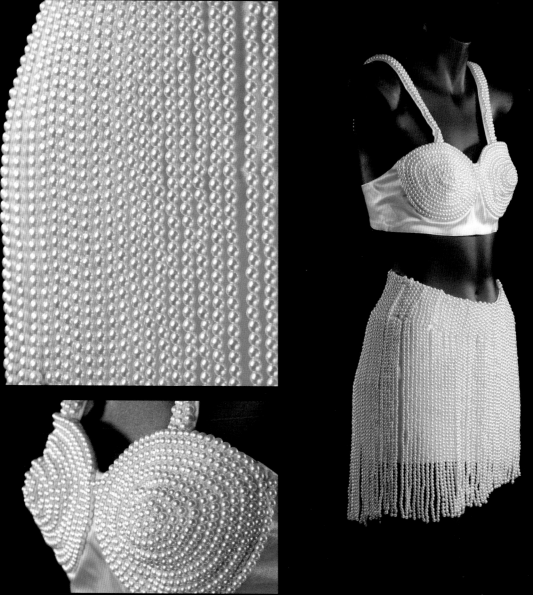

Rhythm of Love photo shoot, 1990

Black suede lace-up ankle boots
Black ribbed stretch cotton bikini
Designed by Azzedine Alaïa [France]

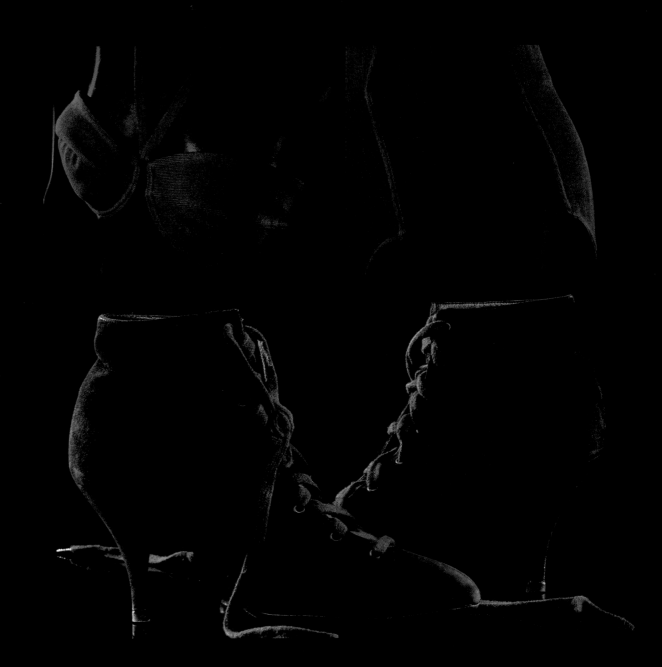

'Better the Devil You Know' video from
the album *Rhythm of Love*, 1990

Video directed by Paul Goldman

Transparent plastic trench coat
Designed by Nicole Bonython [Australia]

Silver lamé hotpants
Designed by Ian McMaugh [Australia]

Three-stranded yellow resin necklace
Dinosaur Designs: Louise Olsen, Stephen
Ormandy and Liane Rossler [Australia]

White sequin lycra bra top
Designer unknown
[Not part of original costume]

'Step Back in Time' video from the
album *Rhythm of Love*, 1990

Video directed by Nick Egan

Vintage peach polyester crêpe dress with
coin trim around neckline and matching belt
Label: Saks Fifth Avenue

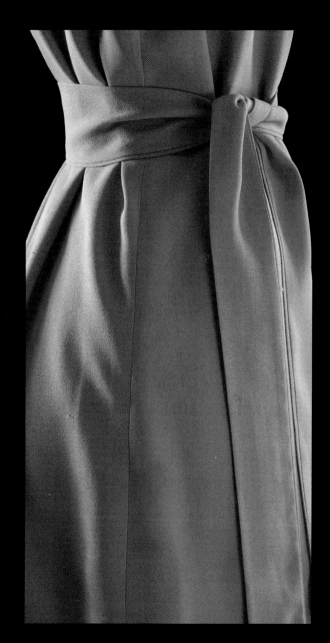

'What Do I Have to Do?' [1991] video
from the album *Rhythm of Love*, 1990

Video directed by David Hogan

Black, polyester crêpe, vintage dress. Side
seams split to hip with white stripe detail
Label: Bon Choix

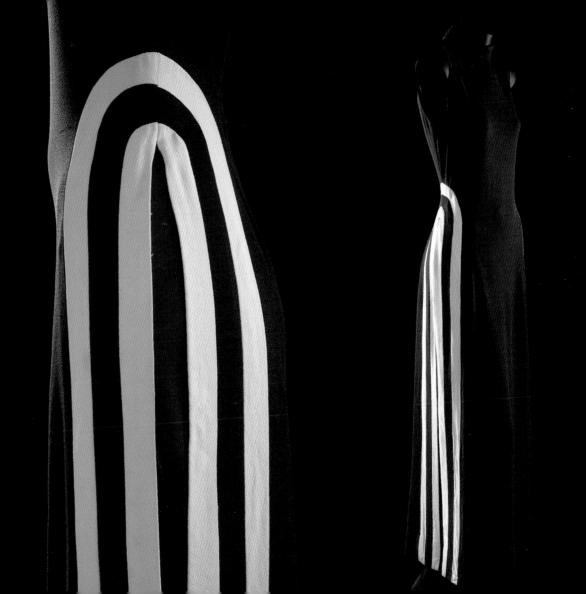

Let's Get To It album cover, 1991

Multi-coloured, vanity print stretch lycra dress
Designed by Nobuhiko Kitamura for
Hysteric Glamour [Japan]

'Finer Feelings' [1992] video from
the *album Let's Get To It*, 1991

Video directed by David Hogan

Black rayon velvet dress and bib trimmed
with black rooster feathers
Designer unknown

'Confide in Me' video from the
album *Kylie Minogue*, 1994

Video directed by Paul Boyd

Camouflage polyester lycra shorts and
matching sleeveless button-up jacket
Label: La Obra

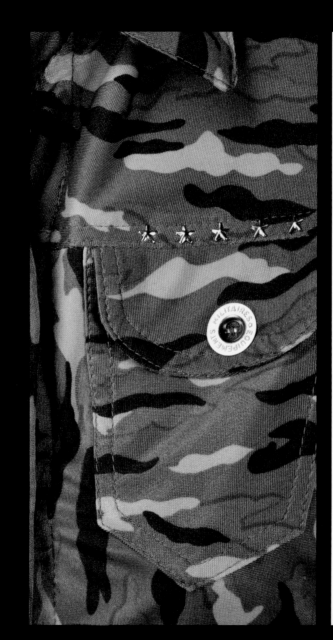

'Confide in Me' video from the
album *Kylie Minogue*, 1994

Video directed by Paul Boyd

Yellow faux fur cropped jacket and
fluorescent orange lycra hotpants
Designer unknown

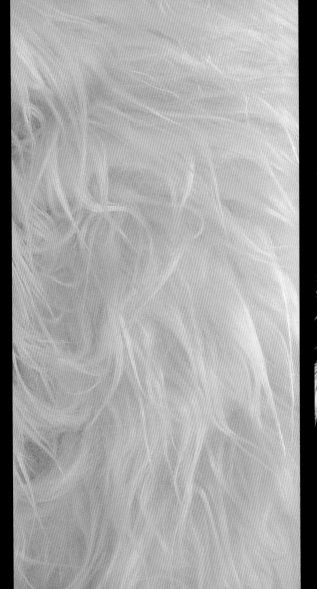

Kylie Minogue album cover, 1994

Green silk taffeta two-piece suit
Paul Smith replica

Impossible Princess album cover, 1998

Blue, black and white nylon and lycra mini dress with
asymmetrical neckline and flared net insert in skirt
Designed by Véronique Leroy [France]

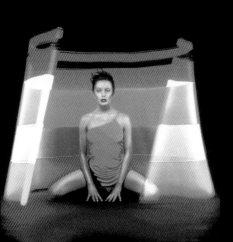

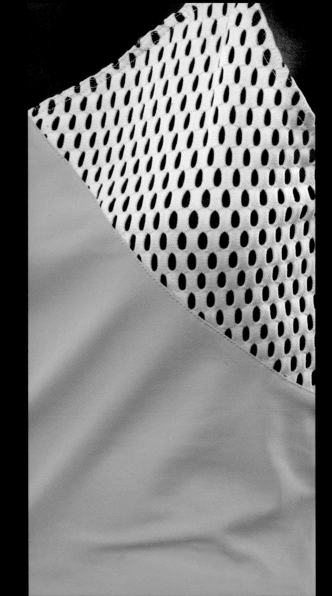

'Did It Again' [1997] video from the
album *Impossible Princess*, 1998

Video directed by Pedro Romanyi

'Sex Kylie' turquoise lycra with black snakeskin
print mini dress with matching waist syncher
Designed by Kylie Minogue, William Baker [UK]
and Stephen Dasilva [UK]

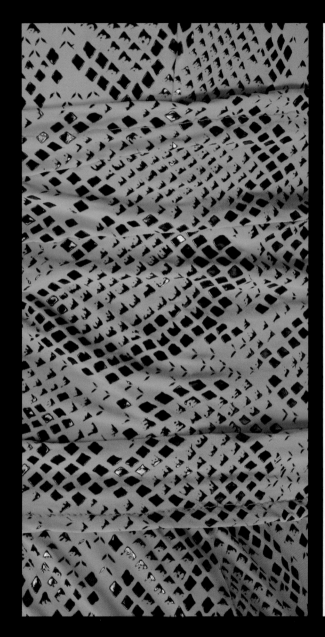

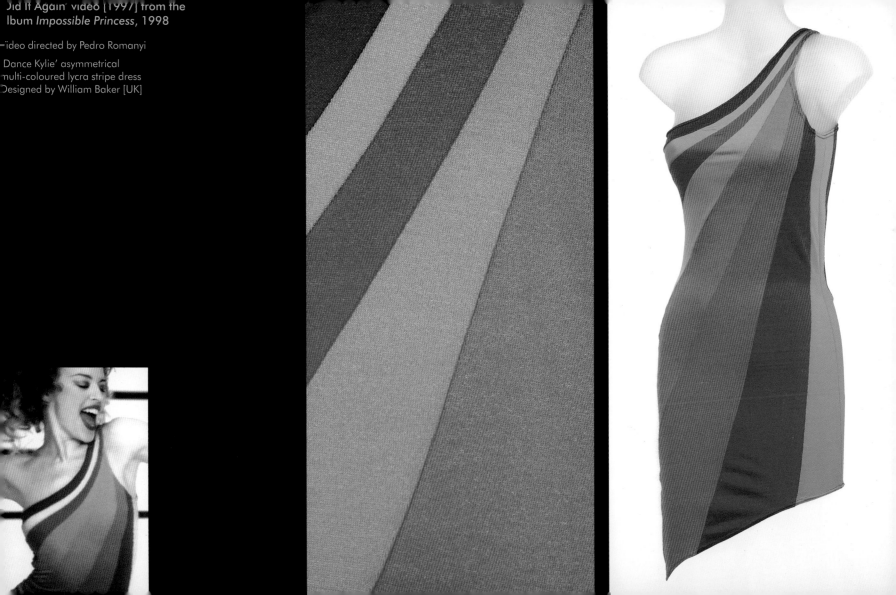

'Did It Again' video [1997] from the
album *Impossible Princess*, 1998

Video directed by Pedro Romanyi

'Dance Kylie' asymmetrical
multi-coloured lycra stripe dress
Designed by William Baker [UK]

'German Bold Italic' video. Single
recorded with Towa Tei, 1998

Video directed by Stephane Sednaoui

Green silk kimono obi and red resin thongs
Purchased in New York

'Spinning Around' video from the
album *Light Years*, 2000

Video directed by Dawn Shadforth

Red silk jersey halter-neck top with nylon
thread choker and metal clasp
Designed by Alexander McQueen [UK]

White cotton drill 'batty rider' shorts
Designed by Stella McCartney [UK] for
Chloé [France]

'Spinning Around' video from the album *Light Years*, 2000

Video directed by Dawn Shadforth

Gold lamé hotpants ruched at sides
Vintage

Worn with gold jersey top with gold
chain neck and back straps
Designed by Stella McCartney [UK]
for Chloé [France]

Gold leather high heel shoes
Label: Gina

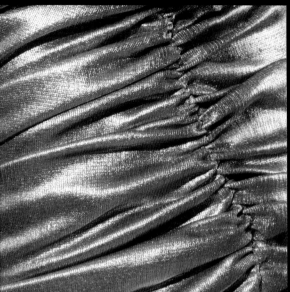

'On a Night Like This' video from
the album *Light Years*, 2000

Video directed by Douglas Avery

Black silk jersey, bias-cut dress with Swarovski
crystal trim and cut-out detail on skirt
Designed by Roland Mouret [France]

'Your Disco Needs You' [2001] video
from the album *Light Years*, 2000

Video directed by Todd Cole

Uncle Sam print brushed cotton
pedal pusher trousers
Designed by Viktor Horsting and Rolf Snoeren
for Viktor and Rolf [France]

Red silk lace body stocking worn as tailcoat
Designed by William Baker [UK]

Red patent 'mock croc' leather
belt with white belt buckle
Designed by Dolce & Gabbana [Italy]

'Can't Get You Out of My Head' video
from the album *Fever*, 2001

Video directed by Dawn Shadforth

White jersey hooded jumpsuit with draped front
opening and extended slits in trousers and sleeves
Designed by Fee Doran for Mrs Jones [UK]

"When I first met Kylie I had just had a
baby and had lost all my confidence.
I was about to haul myself back into
the fashion world with my tail between
my legs when luckily I had the pleasure
of working with William Baker and his
team, which led to working with Kylie.
My tail was between my legs no more.

My son has been obsessed ever since.
He has his own white catsuit, calls
her 'La La La' and will only wear pink!
What can I say about Kylie, apart from
the obvious? She's lovely, and for a
little bird, she's one tough cookie with
a body and face sent from heaven.

As for her style, she could wear
anything and the great thing is that
you don't need much fabric. She
knows exactly what is right for her, and
general conversation in fittings would
consist of either 'higher' or 'lower'.

I will always be grateful to her for giving
an unknown designer a chance, but will
always blame her for my son's 'pinkness'!"

Fee Doran, 2005

'Can't Get You Out of My Head' video
from the album *Fever*, 2001

Video directed by Dawn Shadforth

Lavender halter-neck dress with polyester
satin ribbon tile trim. Based on Gucci design.
Designed by Sandy Gordon [UK]
and Stevie Stewart [UK]

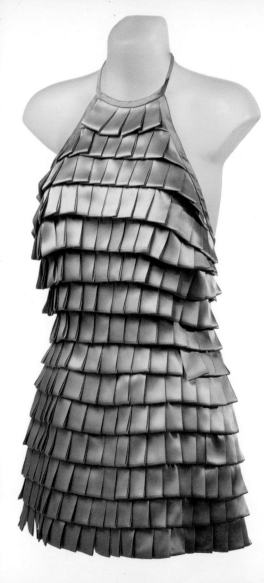

'Come into My World' [2002] video
from the album *Fever*, 2001

Video directed by Michel Gondry

Pink jersey polo T-shirt with black and
white stripe and 'Italia' logo
Black, white and brown wool herringbone trousers
with Dolce & Gabbana logo around waistband
Designed by Dolce & Gabbana [Italy]

Grey suede bag with gold leather
piping and double shoulder strap
Designed by Stella McCartney [UK] for Chloé [France]

'In Your Eyes' [2002] video from
the album *Fever*, 2001

Video directed by Dawn Shadforth

Two-piece multi-coloured leather ribbon
dress with blanket stitch detail
Designed by Fee Doran for Mrs Jones [UK]

Worn with red suede knee-length boots with patent
leather trim [not pictured]
Designed by Dolce & Gabbana [Italy]

'Chocolate' [2004] video from the
album *Body Language*, 2003

Video directed by Dawn Shadforth

Beige gathered chiffon dress with leather detail
Designed by Alexander McQueen [UK]

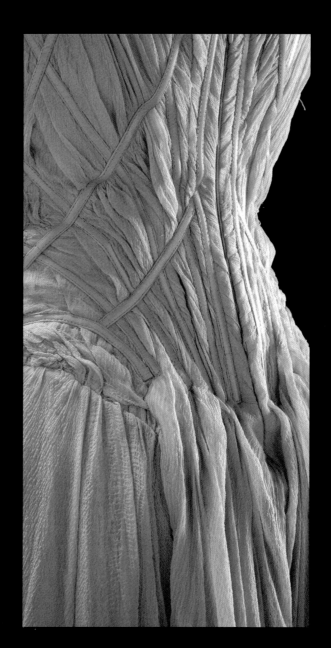

'Chocolate' [2004] video from the
album *Body Language*, 2003

Video directed by Dawn Shadforth

Long red dress with gathered, pleated chiffon
detailing and horsehair panels in skirt
Designed by Helmut Lang Couture [Austria]

Worn with gold painted snakeskin shoes [not pictured]
Designed by Azzedine Alaïa [France]

'Red Blooded Woman' [2004] video from
the album *Body Language*, 2003

Video directed by Jake Nava

Jeans customised with white button and fringe patch
Designed by Pamela Skaist-Levy and Gela Taylor for
Juicy Couture [UK] and customised by Judy Blame [UK]

Black and white woven nylon singlet
Designed by Roland Mouret [France]

Black dyed sheepskin shrug and black satin waist syncher
Designed by William Baker [UK] and Sandy Gordon [UK]

Worn with black leather knee-length boots [not pictured]
Designed by Manolo Blahnik [France]

'I Believe in You' from the album
Ultimate Kylie, 2004

Video directed by Vernie Yeung

Purple chiffon cut-away dress with gold
crystal mesh straps and waistband
Designed by Dolce & Gabbana [Italy]

For Kylie, a live tour offers immense creative freedom. It is the ultimate in performance, a direct dialogue between the audience and herself, a pure transaction of artistic endeavour and appreciation. Outside the constraints of a TV or awards show performance, a live tour offers an opportunity to create a 'world' for the two hours she is on stage. Kylie and her creative team enter into a blank theatre or arena space and transform it. It is like a travelling circus, with up to ten trucks' worth of equipment unloaded for the duration of their stay.

The wardrobe for a live tour holds greater impact when it is designed as a unit. The *Intimate and Live* pink showgirl has more resonance because it follows the minimal severity of Kylie's opening black pedal-pusher suit. The performance takes the audience on a theatrical journey, and the wardrobe amplifies the moods of the songs. Kylie's costumes transform her into different characters and enhance the spectacle for the viewer. A tour wardrobe is full of exaggerated styling such as crystal embellishment, sequins, beads and feathers, as an arena audience could miss subtleties.

Functional factors are a major consideration in tour costume design. Outfits must allow Kylie to perform energetic choreography, while also amplifying her movement through fringing, fluid fabric and form-fitting tailoring. A fast-paced show requires Kylie to change outfits very quickly, with the help of at least three aides. Through dress rehearsals, repetition and experience, many timesaving techniques are put into place, including Velcro, industrial zips and safety catches. Kylie likens the 'quick-change' to a Formula One pit stop.

Doubles of Kylie's stage wardrobe are created to limit wear and tear, and a back-up outfit is always on hand in case of emergency. The demands of a two-hour show on Kylie's body, along with a relentless schedule, mean that her weight changes throughout the duration of a tour. Outfits are constantly re-fitted and altered to ensure a perfect fit and comfort while Kylie is performing.

Kylie's tours have evolved from the bubblegum pop celebration of *Disco In Dreams*, the tongue-in-cheek sexiness of *Let's Get To It*, the pared down determination of *Intimate and Live*, the camp revelation of *On a Night Like This* to the ground-breaking minimal electro dynamism of *KylieFever2002*. The glamorous *Kylie Showgirl: The Greatest Hits Tour* in 2005 pushed this progression even further.

Previous page
On a Night Like This tour, Sydney 2001

Opposite
On a Night Like This tour, Sydney 2001
Kylie's dressing table (left)

KylieFever2002 tour, Elstree, London
Production rehearsals

Disco in Dreams tour [Japan], 1989

Pink stretch polyester satin top trimmed
with sequin braid and matching hotpants
with drop mirror beads
Designed by Ian McMaugh [Australia]

Enjoy Yourself tour
[Australia, United Kingdom,
Europe and Asia], 1990

Blue stretch velvet catsuit with gold
sequin moon and stars appliqué
Designed by Stephen Galloway [Australia]

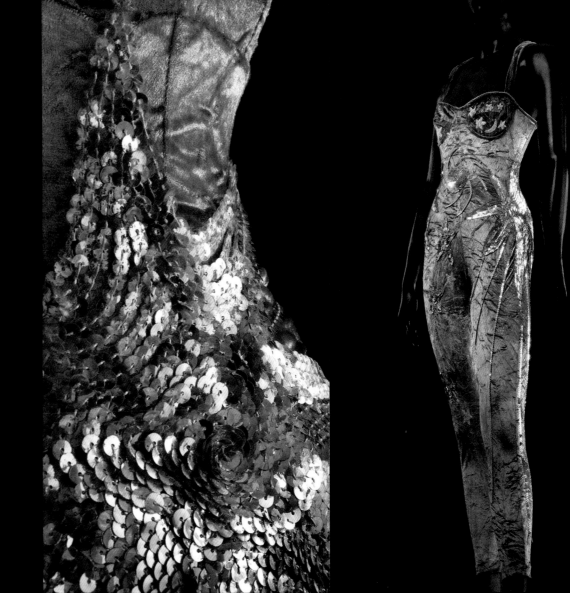

Enjoy Yourself tour
[Australia, United Kingdom,
Europe and Asia], 1990

Blue cotton double-breasted jacket and
shorts with Australian flag motif and
white sequin body suit
Designed by Nicole Bonython [Australia]

Enjoy Yourself tour
[Australia, United Kingdom,
Europe and Asia], 1990

Black lycra catsuit with silver, blue, gold and red
sequin patches to create 'Mondrian' effect
Designed by Ian McMaugh [Australia]

Rhythm of Love tour
[Australia and Asia], 1991

Black PVC bodice with criss-cross straps at back
Label: Rigby and Peller, Knightsbridge [UK]

Black PVC hotpants
Designer unknown

Intimate and Live tour
[Australia and London], 1998

['Dancing Queen']

Pink, silver and white sequin, bugle bead
and fringe 'showgirl' corset
Designed by Kylie Minogue and William Baker [UK]
Realised by Suzanna Burgess [UK]

Pink ostrich feather and diamanté 'showgirl' tiara
Designed and realised by Philip Rhodes [Australia]

"Welcome to Camp Kylie. 'Dancing Queen' was a third of the way into the *Intimate and Live* show, which up until that point was purely song-led without any dancers. But that moment – when the two boys came out in pink sequin hotpants with huge feather backpacks and Kylie stepped forward from behind the glitter-covered 'K', dazzling in showgirl sequins and crowned by a plume of pink feathers – has become the stuff of legend. It was a truly iconic moment: the crowning of the Princess of Pop. In those three minutes two things happened that changed everything that was to come in the next five years: the whole audience cheered and smiled, and Kylie felt immediately at home, and suddenly among that blur of pink feathers and sink sequins, everything seemed to make sense. Kylie was back."

William Baker, 2004

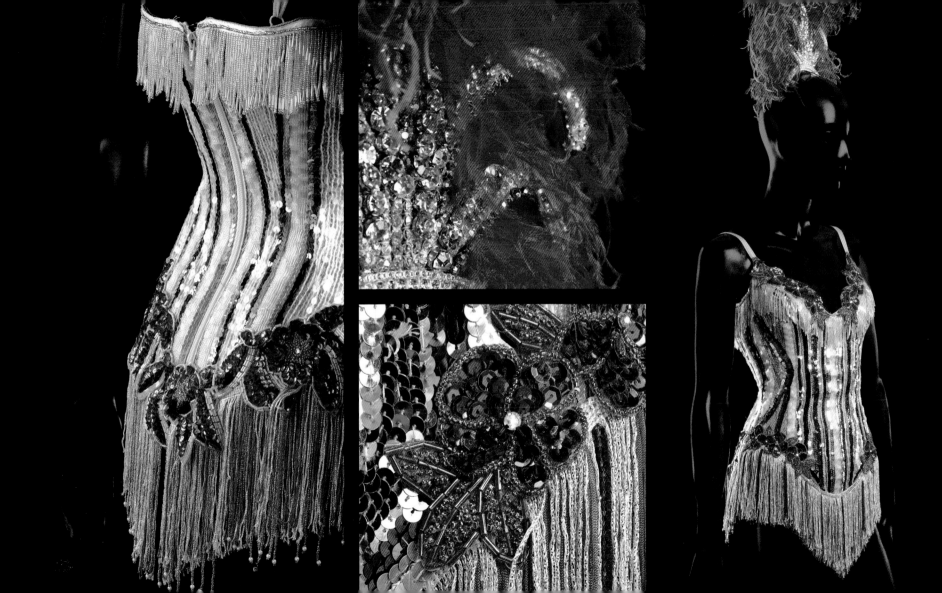

Intimate and Live tour
[Australia and London], 1998

['Cowboy Style']

Blue processed sequin strapless dress
with pink beaded appliqué trim and
fringed hem

Designed by Mark Burnett [Australia]

"Back in 1998, at the humble
beginnings of my career, having
a childhood icon knock at my
door requesting my services was a
complete dream. I remember Kylie
and Will coming over after much
toing-and-froing, and thinking: here
are two incredible people who totally
share my language of bad-is-good-
taste humour. I remember the three of
us dancing around to the (now very
modern) Pointer Sisters, completely
sober and waving glittery fabric
around, while I explained my theory
that you can't go wrong when buying
old records with 'three black sheilas'
on the cover; doesn't matter who they
are! Many a laugh with those two
around. Those were the days ..."

Mark Burnett, 2005

Intimate and Live tour
[Australia and London], 1998

[Encore: 'Confide in Me']

Pistachio satin fringe dress with
V-shaped hem and neckline

Designed by Kylie Minogue and William Baker [UK]
Realised by Suzanna Burgess [UK]

"We had such a small budget to
do the costumes back then, but we
were probably a little ambitious in
matching our ideas with our dress-
making skills. For the 'showgirl'
costume and this fringed dress, we
decided to sew all the sequins and
beading on by hand, thinking it
would only take a couple of days.
Three weeks later and on the other
side of the world we were all sitting
around Kylie's kitchen table with her
Mum and Nan maniacally stitching
sequins and fringing into place. We
eventually realised (in Melbourne)
that we didn't have enough fringing
to complete the dress, so I had
to have some emergency fringing
couriered from London, only to find
when it arrived that it was the wrong
colour. We had to hand-dye it to try
and match the shade, but failed. We
needed the fringing anyway, so the
dress became a two-tone number ..."

William Baker, 2004

Intimate and Live tour
[Australia and London], 1998

[Encore: 'Better the Devil You Know']

Red lamé corset dress with beaded
appliqué and sequin trim
Designed by Mark Burnett [Australia]

Kylie's favourite show shoes, 2000

Opposite

Gold leather shoes with diamanté
trim and gold metal heels
Designed by Manolo Blahnik [UK]

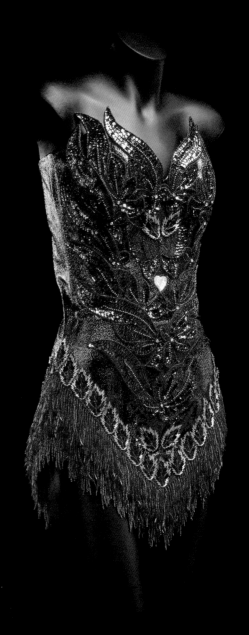

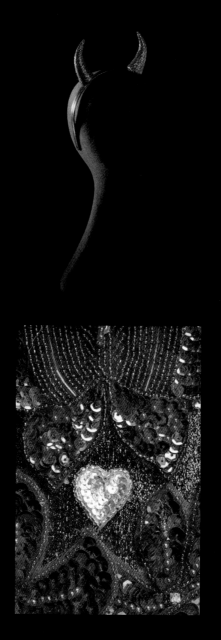

"I went to one of Miss Minogue's shows and I was instantly converted! She is mesmerising; her dress sense communicates her meaning, but even more so, her connection to the public. She is one of the most vibrant figures of our time. Her presentation of self through colours and fabrics absolutely expresses what Kylie is all about – discipline and spontaneity rolled into one! Miss Minogue is very visual; when she comes to my offices she immediately picks up the shoes I think are right for her. I am always completely flattered; it is such a joy when she comes to us."

Mr Manolo Blahnik, 2004

"People are always asking me how I manage to get through a two-hour show in perilous-looking high heels. The answer is simply 'Manolo Blahnik'. I remember buying my first pair of 'Manolo's' well over a decade ago and have been a dedicated fan ever since. I never imagined I would be wearing 'couture show shoes', designed and overseen by the man himself. His designs are feats of engineering: they need to look glamorous but be comfortable and durable. Many pairs have seen me through TV performances, photo shoots, world tours, quick changes, red carpets and more staircases than I can remember. Beyond his talent, he is generous, spirited and a joy to work with."

Kylie Minogue, 2005

On a Night Like This tour
[United Kingdom, Europe
and Australia], 2000

['Loveboat']

Silk embroidered robe with Swarovski crystals
Designed by Julien Macdonald [UK]

"Kylie, the bubbles in champagne – 100%
all woman, wrapped up in a little package
with a big red crystal bow. I have loved
working with Kylie and William over the
years: *On a Night Like This* tour was
fantastic. I spent many a sleepless night
sewing crystals onto Kylie's outfits. There
never seemed to be enough sparkle on
those dainty clothes. She finally nicknamed
me Mr Crystal, obviously pronounced
with a prolonged Welsh accent."

Julien Macdonald, 2004

On a Night Like This tour
[United Kingdom, Europe
and Australia], 2000

['Broadway']

White wool tailcoat and trousers
with white silk waistcoat
Designed by Pamela Blundell [UK]

White mini top hat
Designed by Stephen Jones [UK]

White leather brogue with kitten heel
Designed by Manolo Blahnik [UK]

On a Night Like This tour
[United Kingdom, Europe
and Australia], 2000

['Physical']

Knitted asymmetrical gold dress
with Swarovski crystals
Designed by Julien Macdonald [UK]

Gold leather shoes with diamanté trim
and gold metal heels [pictured on page 71]
Designed by Manolo Blahnik [UK]

On a Night Like This tour
[United Kingdom, Europe
and Australia], 2000

['Butterfly']

Swarovski crystal draped chain bra top
Designed by Julien Macdonald [UK]
Realised by Johnny Rocket [UK]

Gold leather trousers
Designed by Julien Macdonald [UK]

Worn with gold ankle boots [not pictured]
Label: Shellys

On a Night Like This tour [United Kingdom, Europe and Australia], 2000

[Encore: 'Light Years']

Blue and white silk crêpe corset with pleated miniskirt
Designed by Julien Macdonald [UK]

White silk crêpe and blue perspex mini visor
Designed by Stephen Jones [UK]

Blue leather stiletto shoes
Designed by Manolo Blahnik [UK]

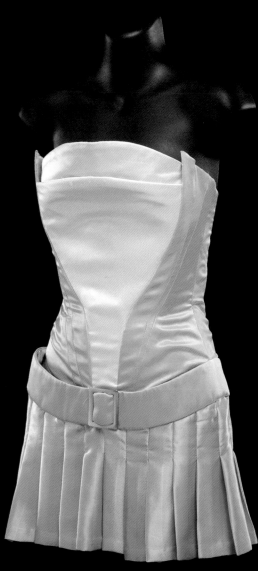

On a Night Like This tour
[United Kingdom, Europe
and Australia], 2000

[Final Encore: 'Spinning Around']

White denim and Swarovski crystal
hotpants worn with jewelled leather belt
Cotton singlet and silk scarf both
covered with Swarovski crystals
Designed by Julien Macdonald [UK]

White nappa leather mule with shocking pink heel
Designed by Manolo Blahnik [UK]

KylieFever2002 **tour**
[United Kingdom, Europe and Australia]

Act One 'Silvanemesis'.
Planet Earth. The Distant Future.

Crystal mesh bra, miniskirt and choker
Designed by Dolce & Gabbana [Italy]

Moulded chrome and silver leather arm bands
Designed by Johnny Rocket [UK]

Silver nappa leather lace-up thigh-length boots
Designed by Jimmy Choo [UK]

"This was a homage to my sci-fi upbringing. Inspired by the Cybermen from BBC's *Doctor Who* and the Borg from *Star Trek*, Kylie's character was based upon a cyber queen flanked by her cyber army, which comprised of 13 dancers in silver lycra with chrome helmets. I wanted Kylie to look regal, sexy and powerful, and this, combined with Rafael Bonachela's almost robotic choreography, achieved a stunning vision of goddess-like perfection."

William Baker, 2004

KylieFever2002 tour
[United Kingdom, Europe and Australia]

Act Two 'Droogie Nights'.
England in the Near Future.

White stretch zip-up jumpsuit, black leather
customised belt and black PVC bra.
Worn with black patent leather knee-length
boots, and silver 'KM' jewellery
Designed by Dolce & Gabbana [Italy]

Black felt bowler hat
Label: Lock and Co. Hatters

Act Four 'Street Style'.
Buffalo, New York, USA, 1982

Stretch satin shirt with fluorescent trim, navy
cotton drill hipster trousers with braces, white mesh
'Slim Lady' singlet and fluorescent orange bra.
Worn with customised police hat, fingerless leather
gloves, gold 'KM' jewellery and black leather ankle
boots [not pictured]
Designed by Dolce & Gabbana [Italy]

KylieFever2002 tour
[United Kingdom, Europe and Australia]

Act Three 'The Crying Game'. Hollywood, 1940

Black silk corset dress with black lacing
at sides and antique lace panels
Designed by Dolce & Gabbana [Italy]

KylieFever2002 tour
[United Kingdom, Europe and Australia]

Act Five 'Sex in Venice'.
Venice, Italy. Late Eighteenth Century

Gold stretch satin corset and knickers trimmed
with black lace and ribbon.
Black lace wrist ruffs and loop earrings
Designed by Dolce & Gabbana [Italy]

Black polka dot patent leather
peep-toe shoes with bows
Designed by Agent Provocateur

"It was a great experience to work
with Kylie on the *KylieFever2002* tour.
She is such an eclectic and fabulous
personality on stage, that designing
her tour wardrobe was a really
exciting and fun challenge. It also
allowed us to get to know her and we
enjoyed the fittings. She is extremely
sweet, but also the consummate
professional and a hard worker.
We shared ideas and her input was
always welcome, but at the end of
the day she is the one who has to go
on stage, and needs to feel at ease
besides looking gorgeous and sexy."

Dolce & Gabbana, 2004

KylieFever2002 tour
[United Kingdom, Europe and Australia]

Act Six 'Cybertronica'. Cyberspace.
An Alternate Timeline. About Now.

White cotton drill combat trousers with fluorescent
details. Flurorescent 'KM' bangles. Worn with
fluorescent pink and white ankle boots [not pictured]
Designed by Dolce & Gabbana [Italy]

Pink stretch jersey asymmetrical
tanktop with quilted collar detail
Designed by Cyberdog

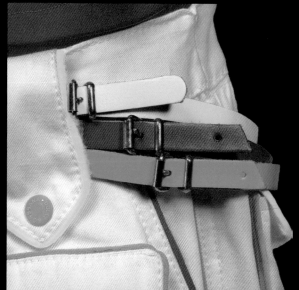

KylieFever2002 tour
[United Kingdom, Europe and Australia]

Encore: 'Voodooinferno'

Black woven mini dress with orange feather trim
braid and loose strips of leather and beading.
Gold hoop earrings with feathers attached
and gold vinyl thigh-length leather
boots with leopard-print lining

Designed by Dolce & Gabbana [Italy]

KylieFever2002 tour
[United Kingdom, Europe and Australia]

Encore

Cream cotton waistcoat and beige needle
corduroy combat trousers with brown
leather trim.
Worn with white cotton trilby with white
grosgrain ribbon and yellow nappa
'Banana' stilettos
Designed by Dolce & Gabbana [Italy]

"I think this was one of the most
successful looks Dolce & Gabbana
did for us. Kylie originally paired the
'Banana' stilettos with the combat pants
for the video for 'Love at First Sight'
(combined with my house keys around
her neck), and it was so popular that
weeks later the high street was full of
rip-offs, girls everywhere imitating the
look. Everyone wanted those trousers.
Dolce & Gabbana glamorised workwear.
We used to call it farmer chic …"

William Baker, 2004

Kylie Showgirl: The Greatest Hits Tour, 2005
[United Kingdom and Europe]

Act One 'Showgirl'. A Deco Revue.

Head dress of blue and white ostrich
feathers and star-shaped Swarovski crystals
with blue satin base and ribbon ties
Designed by John Galliano [UK]

Blue satin halter-neck corset embroidered
with star-shaped Swarovski crystals and
sequins with flesh-coloured inserts at hips
Designed by John Galliano [UK]

Blue and white ostrich feather bustle with spray of
star-shaped Swarovski crystals on wire stems
Designed by John Galliano [UK]

Kylie has been a friend for a long
time and I have always admired
her for her talent, professionalism
and personal style. Now I can also
say that she is the bravest and
most positive person I know.

This is the second time that we
have had the pleasure to work
together and like the first time it
is a fabulous experience. It leaves
you enriched. She knows exactly
what she wants and goes for it.
She is hard working but fun loving.
Kylie is the last true showgirl.

John Galliano, 2006

Kylie Showgirl: The Greatest Hits Tour, 2005
[United Kingdom and Europe]

Act Five 'Dreams'. A Sound Stage.
Hollywood, USA. The Thirties.

Pale pink chiffon, fitted dress with Swarovski
crystal covered shoe string straps and V-shaped
insert. Trimmed with clusters of clear glass
beads, Swarovski crystals and ostrich feathers
Designed by Karl Lagerfeld [for Chanel Couture]

THE PERFORMANCES

The global reach of TV awards shows allows for a more elaborate stage production in which to promote a song. Kylie's live versions of 'Can't Get You Out of My Head' at the MTV Europe Music Awards in 2001 and the BRIT Awards in 2002 are two of her most memorable TV awards performances. Kylie's rendition of 'Dancing Queen', as part of the Sydney 2000 Olympic Games Closing Ceremony, was an iconic moment in her career.

The flip side of these larger-than-life interpretations is the great number of smaller one-off gigs that can be found dotted throughout Kylie's career. Any Kylie show, big or small, is adapted to suit the particular venue and occasion. One intimate venue to which she has returned time and again is the nightclub G-A-Y at the London Astoria. The experience of an ever-faithful crowd going wild in such a venue is unlike anything else. Kylie enjoys the challenge of random or unexpected gigs, where she has to draw upon all her experience, responding to a different crowd to present the best show possible.

A costume that has not been specially designed for a live performance usually needs to be adapted before its turn in the spotlight. All eventualities are considered before Kylie steps onto the stage – shoe soles are rubbered, tassels sewn out of the way of zips, and straps secured. In the minutes before she leaves her dressing room Kylie is surrounded by her wardrobe team in an intense 'lockdown' period. Final checks are carried out to ensure that everything is stitched into place for safety and modesty.

With wind machines, slippery floors, flash photography, dance manoeuvres, quick changes and any other element that decides to present itself, the golden rule is to expect the unexpected.

Previous page

MTV Europe Music Awards, Festhalle, Frankfurt, Germany, 8 November 2001

White chiffon asymmetrical Grecian dress with matching chiffon hood. Black leather belt with gold-plated logo letters [detail]. Designed by Dolce & Gabbana [Italy]

This page

'Dancing Queen', Olympic Games Closing Ceremony, Olympic Stadium, Sydney, 1 October 2000

'Rhythm of Life' Fashion Charity Gala,
Grosvenor Hotel, London, June 1992

White cotton singlet with paper trim
and girdle skirt with chiffon strips
Designed by John Galliano [UK]

Sydney Gay and Lesbian Mardi Gras
Party, Royal Hall of Industries, Sydney
Showgrounds, 5 March 1994

Pink silk corset dress with feather
skirt and mirror heart trim
Designed by Xen Pardoe Miles [Australia]

Stonewall Equality Show. Duet with Elton John,
Royal Albert Hall, London, 22 October 1995

Pale mint-green crop top and hotpants
covered with layers of beaded fringing
Designed by Antonio Berardi (Italy)

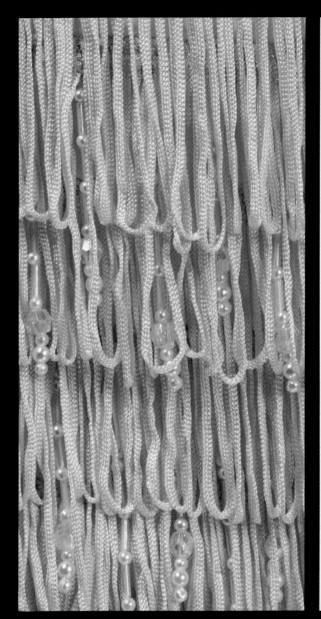

White silk mini dress with cut-away back,
trimmed with silver beaded fringing
Designed by Antonio Berardi [Italy]

'Where the Wild Roses Grow' with
Nick Cave and The Bad Seeds,
Top of The Pops, BBC Television,
London, October 1995

Green devoré silk, bias-cut slip
dress with 'beetle' detail
Designed by Owen Gaster [UK]

"Kylie wore this dress for a performance
of 'Where the Wild Roses Grow' with
Nick Cave on *Top of the Pops.* This was
the first TV appearance that I worked
on with Kylie and all the styling was
directly inspired by her character in the
song – the ill-fated murder victim, Eliza
Day. At the time, Owen Gaster was
one of a new wave of young English
designers reviving the flagging British
fashion scene. He combined ingenious
pattern-cutting techniques and an avant-
garde design ethic with a flamboyant
theatricality. This simple dress seemed
perfect to bring Eliza Day to life, with
its bright green devoré beetles crawling
over a delicate bias-cut sheath of chiffon.
It has always been important to us that
Kylie promotes and wears young and
emerging fashion talent ... They often
possess an originality and usually 'raw'
sense of glamour that separates them
from many of their more seasoned
and well-known contemporaries."

William Baker, 2004

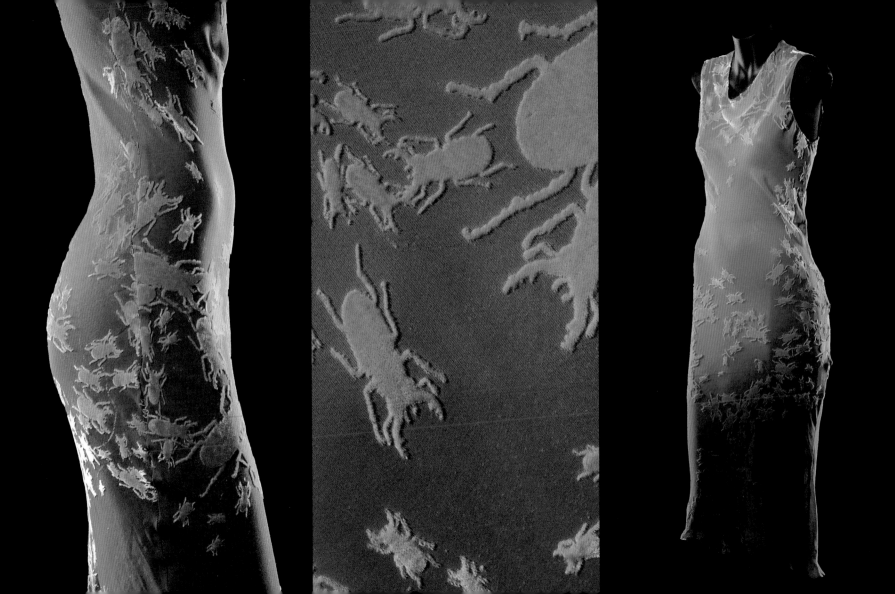

Hot pink chiffon halter-neck rouched dress
Designed by Veronique Leroy [France]

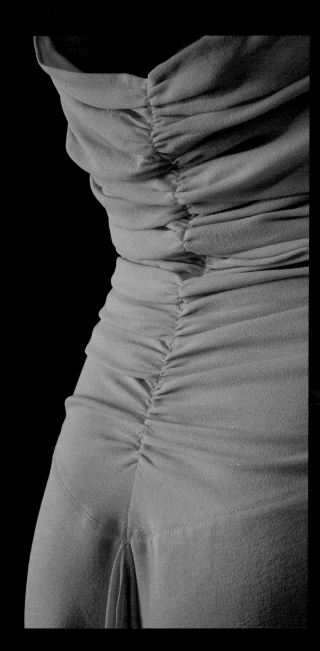

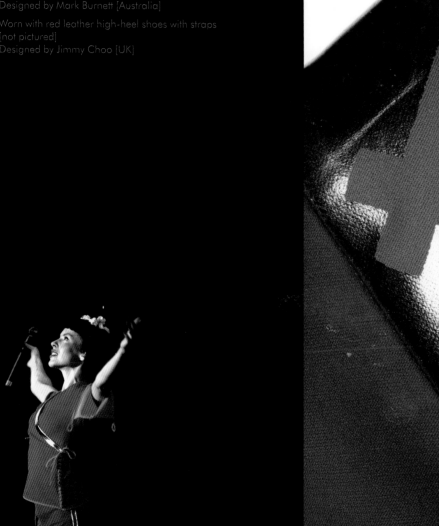

*Mushroom 25, Melbourne Cricket Ground,
14 November 1998*

Red Japanese polyester tracksuit with hot pink
piping and buttons, and silver foil collar
Designed by Mark Burnett [Australia]

Worn with red leather high-heel shoes with straps
[not pictured]
Designed by Jimmy Choo [UK]

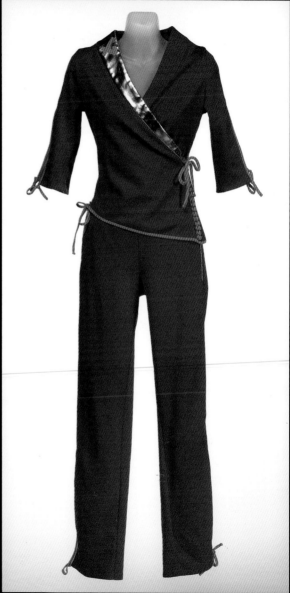

Long gold sequin mesh dress with
halter-neck and gold metal trim
Designed by Michael Wilkinson [Australia]

Worn with gold leather T-bar shoes
with diamante trim [not pictured]
Designed by Gina [UK]

Gold PVC trousers and halter-neck corset
top with gold-plated chains and studs
Designed by Michael Wilkinson [Australia]
Realised by Julie Bryant [Australia]

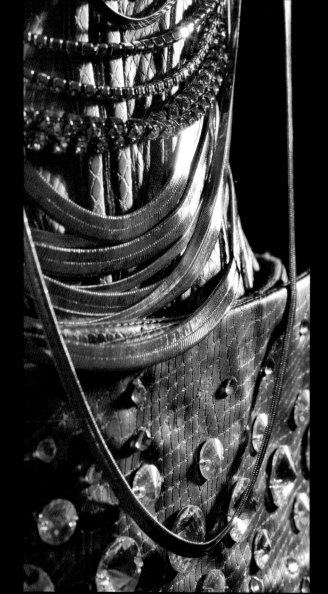

Smash Hits Poll Winners Party,
London Arena, London, 9 December 2001

Blue denim jeans encrusted with coloured
sequins, stones and Swarovski crystals
Designed by Julien Macdonald [UK]

White stretch cotton, screen-printed singlet with
Swarovski crystal trim and zip detail [not pictured]
Designed by Chloé [UK]

An Audience with Kylie television special,
ITV Network, London, 22 September 2001

Black ribbon tile corset with crystal bugle bead fringe
Designed by William Baker [UK],
Stevie Stewart [UK] and Sandy Gordon [UK]

Dyed polyester georgette cape with leather
straps at neck, wrist and ankles
Designed by Fee Doran for Mrs Jones [UK]

Winged head dress with black and oilskin
feathers and black Swarovski crystals
Designed by Stephen Jones [UK]

An Audience with Kylie television special,
ITV Network, London, 22 September 2001

Red jersey strapless jumpsuit with front leg splits
and red leather wrist bands, belt and bow tie
Designed by Fee Doran for Mrs Jones [UK]

Worn with red felt trilby with sequin
bow and feather trim [opposite]
Leopard print faux fur trilby with appliqué trim
Black mesh trilby with red and pink diamantés
Designed by Cosmo Jenks [UK]

KylieFever2002 tour, end of tour party,
Milan, 11 June 2002

Gold lamé asymmetrical top and miniskirt with
matching visor
Leather belt with coins attached and coin arm bands
Designed by Dolce & Gabbana [Italy]

MTV Europe Music Awards, Festhalle,
Frankfurt, Germany, 8 November 2001

White chiffon asymmetrical Grecian dress.
Black leather belt with gold plated logo letters

Worn with matching chiffon hood and white leather
high-heel shoes with multiple straps and gold ring
[not pictured]
Designed by Dolce & Gabbana [Italy]

White string vest dress woven through with
multi-coloured leather fringe pieces
Designed by Fee Doran for Mrs Jones [UK]

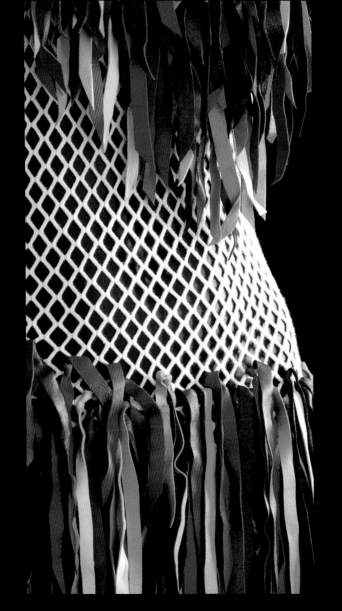

BRIT Awards, Earl's Court,
London, 20 February 2002

White stretch cotton mini corset dress with
flesh-coloured lace-up side panel
Designed by Dolce & Gabbana [Italy]

'K' logo designed by Tony Hung [UK]
Personalised sterling silver 'K' tag jewellery
Designed by Johnny Rocket [UK]

Peach cotton jersey mini dress with
bronze square sequin panel
Designed by Rafael Lopez [Spain]

BRIT Awards, Earls Court,
London, 20 February 2003

Black silk jersey mini dress with Swarovski
crystal collar and back straps
Designed by Julien Macdonald [UK]

"I remember a night ... It was around
three a.m. when my phone rang. It was
Kylie and she desperately needed a
dress for the BRIT Awards for a surprise
duet with Justin Timberlake. The whole
performance had changed and she
couldn't dance in the dress they had
prepared. It was also the day of my show
and I had only one thing – a couture
crystal gown that literally went straight
from the catwalk into William's bag.
Kylie loved it. As I watched the BRITs
that night my heart stopped! Kylie and
William had cut the dress in half and
made it into a mega mini!! Kylie did
look fantastic and it made all the front
pages the next day, so all was forgiven."

Julien Macdonald, 2004

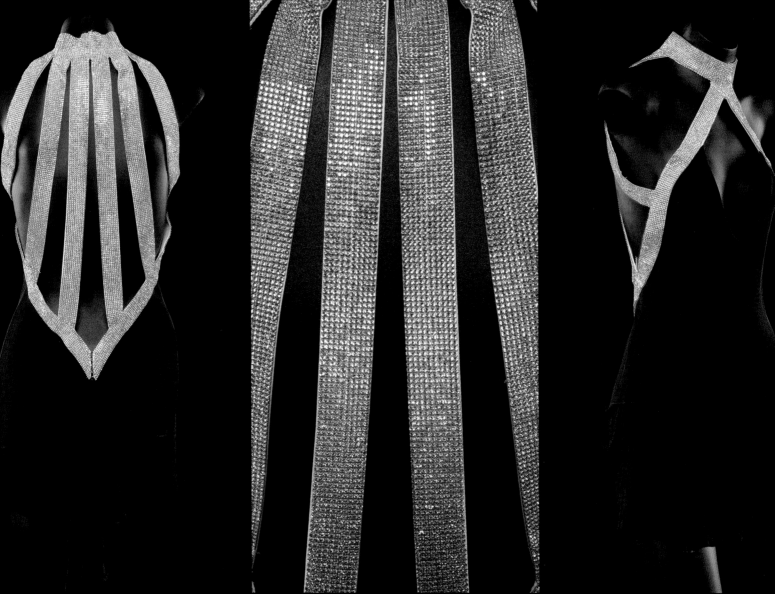

Top of the Pops, BBC Television, London,
28 November 2003

Cotton button-up romper suit and perspex
platform shoes studded with Swarovski crystals
Designed by Emilio Pucci [Italy]

Transparent PVC waist syncher studded
with Swarovski crystals
Designed by William Baker [UK]
and Sandy Gordon [UK]

"I met Kylie in London over a cappuccino
after her facial. It was a fun, easy
meeting, like getting together with
someone you've known forever. I liked
her immediately: her passion for Pucci
(and my passion for anyone who loves
Pucci), all that personality in a perfectly
proportioned body and a big smile. She
overwhelmed me with her warmth and
enthusiasm. I smile when I listen to her
CDs and remember that first meeting."

Laudomia Pucci, Image Director,
Emilio Pucci, 2004

Money Can't Buy concert,
Carling Apollo Theatre, Hammersmith,
London, 15 November 2003

Breton striped wool cropped sweater
Designed by Jean Paul Gaultier [France]

Black stretch high-waisted leggings with
black button side detail
Designed by Stevie Stewart for Bodymap [UK]

Black silk waist 'syncher
Designed by William Baker [UK]

Worn with black suede peep-toe shoes [not pictured]
Designed by Vivienne Westwood [UK]

Money Can't Buy concert,
Carling Apollo Theatre, Hammersmith,
London, 15 November 2003

Three-tone cotton jersey four-piece dress with
metallic leather side pouch and black cotton jersey
arm band
Designed by Helmut Lang [Austria]

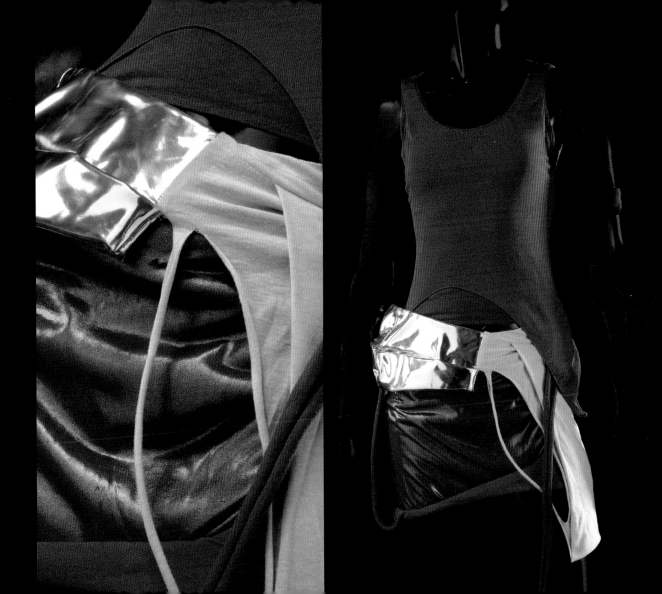

Money Can't Buy concert,
Carling Apollo Theatre, Hammersmith,
London, 15 November 2003

White jersey panelled catsuit with white silk waist
syncher, studded with Swarovski crystals
Designed by Stevie Stewart for Bodymap [UK]

Bicycle chain and white tassel belt
Designed by Judy Blame [UK]

Worn with white leather
knee-length boots [not pictured]
Designed by Manolo Blahnik [UK]

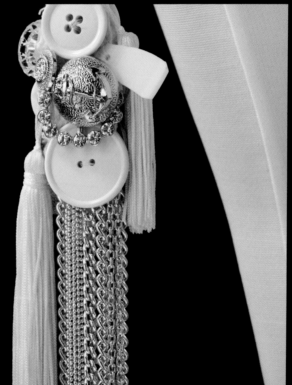

Black satin customised corset and shoelace and
chain belt with mixed buttons and charms
Designed by Judy Blame [UK]

Black crinkle silk chiffon and diamanté
wraparound skirt
Designed by Edward Meadham [UK]

Worn with black silk top hat with Swarovski
crystal band [not pictured]
Designed by Stephen Jones [UK]

THE RED CARPET

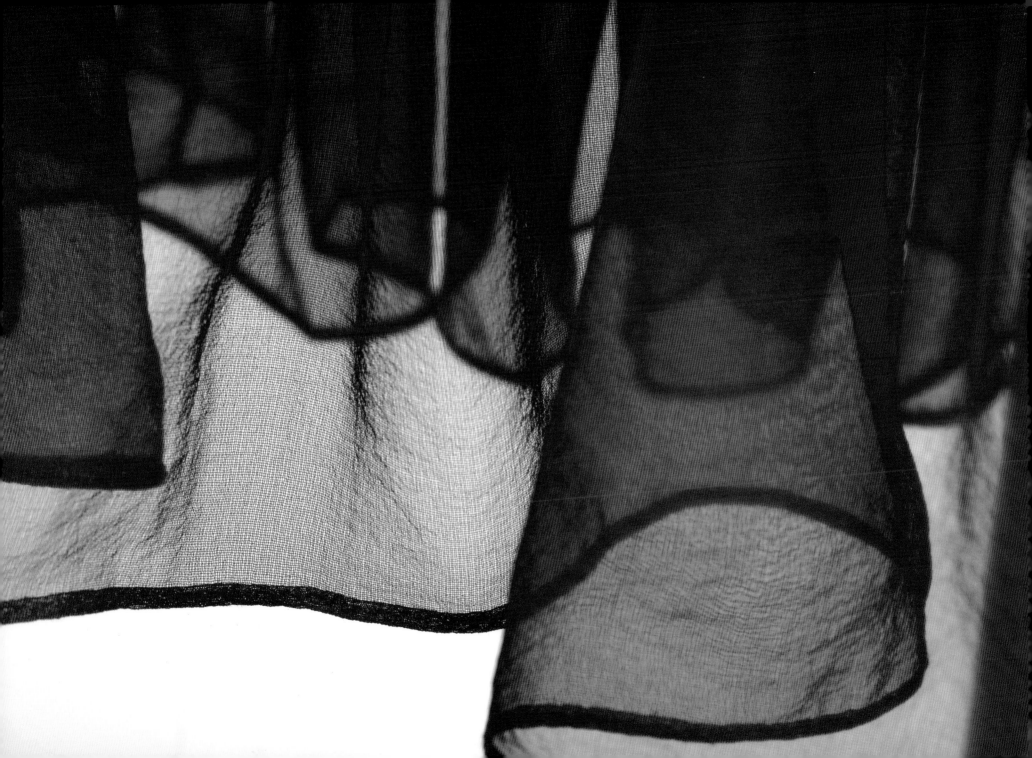

As the culture of celebrity has intensified over the past decade, so too has the power of paparazzi photography. Red carpet images travel incredibly fast from the photographer's digital camera to the press, via the internet. These images get their first viewing in the tabloid press, before weekly gossip magazines offer their verdict, and the fashion press illustrates emerging trends. The amusing and telling offshoot of these images comes several weeks later when the fast-moving high street stores start selling replica versions of celebrity clothes.

Competition for designer dresses is fierce. Female celebrities all over the world turn to the same handful of designers to make them dazzle on the red carpet. People look to Kylie as a style icon, so many of the world's foremost designers are eager for her to be the first to appear in their latest creation.

As well as working with the world's elite, Kylie has always felt it important to support emerging young designers. She has worn outfits direct from fashion students' graduation collections, or that have come straight off the sewing machine in their bedroom.

Vintage dresses are used in the same way. Kylie can count on several sources throughout Europe, who are constantly on the lookout for suitable vintage outfits.

Whatever the choice – established or emerging designer or vintage – it's important to have a sense of experimentation and enjoy the discovery of the unexpected.

Previous page
Laureus Sports Awards, Grimaldi Forum, Monaco, 20 May 2003

Red, ruched silk jersey dress with necktie [detail]
Designed by Giambattista Valli for Emmanuel Ungaro [France]

This page
MTV Europe Music Awards, Ocean Terminal Arena, Edinburgh, Scotland, 6 November 2003

Silver leather shoes with jewel trim [detail]
Designed by Dolce & Gabbana [Italy]

Brown jersey panelled dress with pink chiffon skirt
and fishtail trimmed with brown satin ribbon.
Designed by Gursel Ali [Australia] with Kylie Minogue.
Realised by Jean Ali [Australia].

Moulin Rouge! premiere, Odeon Cinema, Leicester Square, London. 3 September 2001

Black net dress with black sequins and antique flesh-coloured lace panels
Designed by Collette Dinnigan [Australia]

"I felt the dress was perfect for the event. Kylie looked gorgeous and was the perfect person to wear such a sensual, feminine dress. She in herself provides great inspiration and the event was the ideal place for Kylie to shine."

Collette Dinnigan, 2004

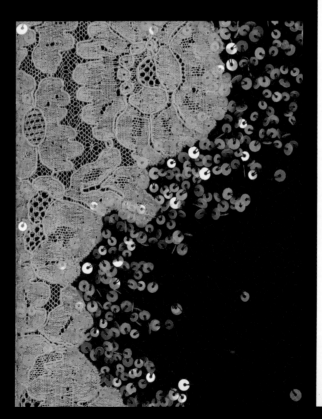

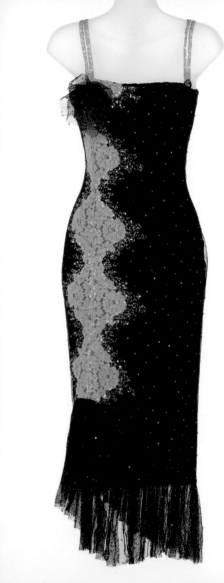

KylieFever2002 tour
[United Kingdom, Europe and Australia]

After concert birthday party,
Wembley Arena, 27 May 2002

Cream silk floor-length vintage dress with
slashed sleeves and gold trim at waist
Designed by Frank Usher (UK)

"Throughout her career it has
always been obvious that Kylie has
a unique knowledge of vintage
clothing, along with a great ability
to interpret rather than impersonate,
giving a modern twist on classic
icons such as Elizabeth Taylor
wearing vintage Frank Usher Grecian
goddess or her Brigitte Bardotesque
look, each time giving it her own
stamp of individuality. I don't think
there's anything in fashion that
would be too much for our Kylie."

Steven Phillips, Co-owner
Rellik Vintage Boutique, 2004

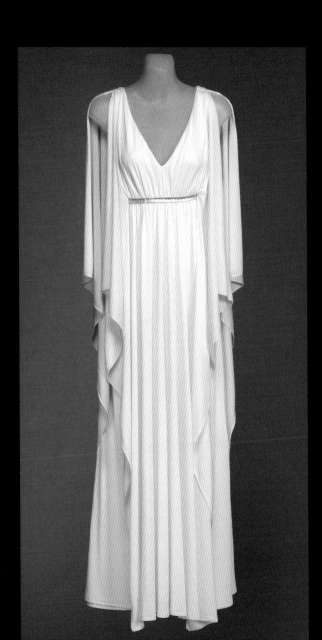

16th Annual ARIA Awards, Superdome,
Homebush Bay, Sydney, 15 October 2002

White silk, long dress with asymmetrical
neckline and low back trimmed with bands
of Swarovski crystals
Designed by Julien Macdonald (UK)

Pale pink leather buckle hipster trousers
and silver mesh layered singlet tops
Designed by Dolce & Gabbana (Italy)

BRIT Awards, Earl's Court,
London, 20 February 2003

Oyster pink stretch satin dress with
flesh-coloured lacing at sides
Designed by Dolce & Gabbana (Italy)

Worn with pink perspex visor and
Swarovski crystal cuff
Designed by Scott Wilson (UK)

Sterling silver 'JT' heart logo chain and earrings
Designed by Johnny Rocket (UK)

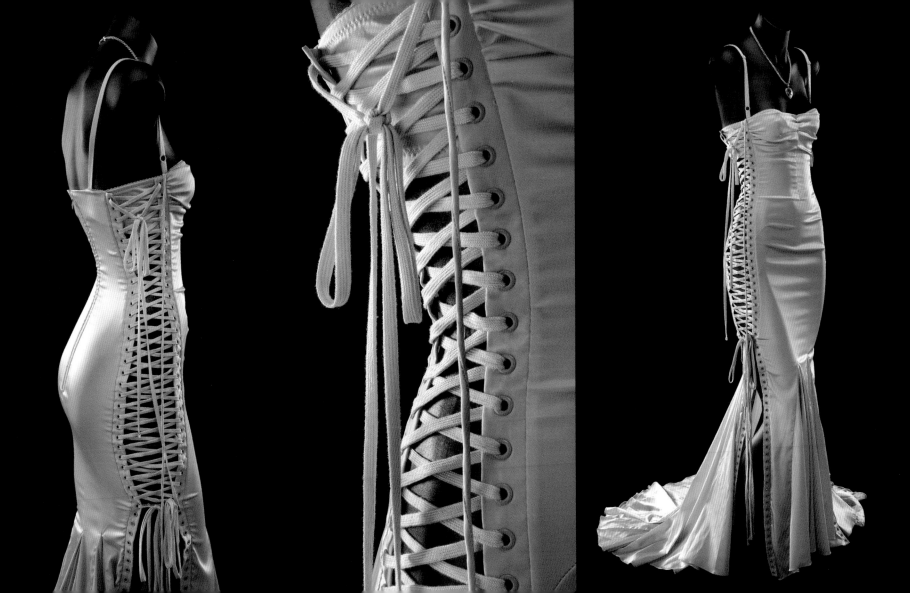

Royal Variety Performance,
Carling Apollo Theatre, Hammersmith,
London, 2 December 2002

Blue silk fringe dress draped from
centre front to centre back seam.
Designed by Rafael Lopez (Spain)

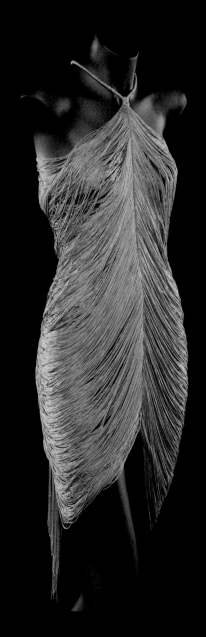

Laureus Sports Awards,
Grimaldi Forum, Monaco, 20 May 2003

Red, ruched silk jersey dress with necktie
Designed by Giambattista Valli for
Emanuel Ungaro (France)

Ivor Novello Awards, Le Meridien
Grosvenor House, London, 22 May 2003

Black and white wool dress.
Monogrammed leather belt featuring
chain and pearl attachment.
Designed by Karl Lagerfeld
for Chanel (France)

"Kylie is like a small doll with a
perfect body. She has a strong,
interesting personality. I really
love her! I love the way she wears
clothes; she is stylish, and I love
the way she wears Chanel - very
personal, so sexy and rock 'n' roll."

Karl Lagerfeld, 2004

MTV Video Music Awards, Radio City
Music Hall, New York, 29 August 2003

White jersey drape dress with
crystal-studded star brooch
Designed by Giambattista Valli for
Emmanuel Ungaro (France)

"Her proportions are amazing,
simply perfect, literally inviting
you to drape jersey around her
body. This is how we created the
white dress: directly on her."

Giambattista Valli for
Emmanuel Ungaro, 2004

MTV Europe Music Awards
Ocean Terminal Arena, Edinburgh,
Scotland, 6 November 2003

Green chiffon empire-line dress with
jewelled trim
Silver leather shoes with jewel trim
Designed by Dolce & Gabbana (Italy)

46th Annual Grammy Awards,
Staples Centre, Los Angeles, 8 February 2004

Pale pink, silk jersey and net layered dress
Designed by Martine Sitbon [France]

Echo German Music Awards,
International Congress Centre,
Berlin, 6 March 2004

Black and flesh-coloured lace corset
dress with knitted 'shrug' top
Designed by Alexander McQueen [UK]

THE FINALE

COSTUME COLLECTION CHECKLIST

The Kylie Minogue Collection comprises over 600 costumes and accessories. A selection of them feature in the *KYLIE* catalogue.

The checklist includes all the costumes and accessories that appear in the catalogue. Costumes and accessories that appear in the Australian and UK tour of *Kylie – The Exhibition* have been selected from this checklist.

Designers

Azzedine Alaïa, born Tunisia, 1940
Rhythm of Love photo shoot, 1990
Black suede lace-up ankle boots
Black ribbed stretch cotton bikini

'Chocolate' [2004] video from the album *Body Language*, 2003
Gold painted snakeskin leather shoes

Gursel Ali, born UK, 1960
TV Week Logie Awards, Hyatt On Collins Ballroom, Melbourne, March 1989
Brown jersey panelled dress with pink chiffon skirt and fishtail trimmed with brown satin ribbon
Co-designed with Kylie Minogue. Realised by Jean Ali [Australia]

William Baker, born UK, 1974
'Did It Again' video [1997] from the album *Impossible Princess*, 1998
'Sex Kylie'
Turquoise lycra with black snakeskin print mini dress with matching waist syncher
Co-designed with Kylie Minogue and Stephen Dasilva

'Dance Kylie'
Asymmetrical multicoloured lycra stripe dress

Intimate and Live tour [Australia and London], 1998
['Dancing Queen']
Pink, silver and white sequin, bugle bead and fringe 'showgirl' corset
Co-designed with Kylie Minogue. Realised by Suzanna Burgess [UK]

[Encore: 'Confide In Me']
Pistachio satin fringe dress with V-shaped hem and neckline
Co-designed with Kylie Minogue. Realised by Suzanna Burgess [UK]

'Your Disco Needs You' [2001] video from the album *Light Years*, 2000
Red silk lace body stocking worn as a tailcoat

An Audience With Kylie television special, ITV Network, London, 22 September 2001
Black ribbon tile corset with crystal bugle bead fringe
Co-designed with Stevie Stewart and Sandy Gordon

'Red Blooded Woman' [2004] video from the album *Body Language*, 2003
Black dyed sheepskin shrug and black satin waist syncher
Co-designed with Sandy Gordon

Money Can't Buy concert, Carling Apollo Theatre, Hammersmith, London, 15 November 2003
Black silk waist syncher

Top of the Pops, BBC Television, 28 November 2003
Transparent PVC waist syncher studded with Swarovski crystals
Co-designed with Sandy Gordon

Jenny Bannister, born Australia, 1954
'I Should Be So Lucky' [1987] video from the album *Kylie*, 1988
White cotton muslin dress with over-sized pocket detail

Antonio Berardi, born UK, 1968
Stonewall Equality Show. Duet with Elton John, Royal Albert Hall, London, 22 October 1995
Pale mint-green crop top and hotpants covered with layers of beaded fringing

G-A-Y at the London Astoria, 25 June 1995
White silk mini dress with cut-away back, trimmed with silver beaded fringing

Manolo Blahnik, born Canary Islands, 1942
'Did It Again' video [1997] from the album *Impossible Princess*, 1998
Red suede mules with fringe trim

On a Night Like This tour [United Kingdom, Europe and Australia], 2000
['Broadway']
White leather brogue with kitten heel

['Physical']
Gold leather shoes with diamanté trim and gold metal heels

[Encore: 'Light Years']
Blue leather stiletto shoes

[Final Encore: 'Spinning Around']
White nappa leather mule with shocking pink heel

Money Can't Buy concert, Carling Apollo Theatre, Hammersmith, London, 15 November 2003
White leather knee-length boots

'Red Blooded Woman' [2004] video from the album *Body Language*, 2003
Black leather knee-length boots

Judy Blame, born UK
'Red Blooded Woman' [2004] video from the album *Body Language*, 2003
Jeans customised with white button and fringe patch
Label: Juicy Couture [UK]

Money Can't Buy concert, Carling Apollo Theatre, Hammersmith, London, 15 November 2003
Bicycle chain and white tassel belt

G-A-Y at the London Astoria, 28 February 2004
Black satin customised corset and shoelace and chain belt with mixed buttons and charms

Pamela Blundell, born UK
On a Night Like This tour [United Kingdom, Europe and Australia], 2000
['Broadway']
White wool tailcoat and trousers with white silk waistcoat

Nicole Bonython, born Australia, 1962
'Better the Devil You Know' video from the album *Rhythm of Love*, 1990
Transparent plastic trench coat

Enjoy Yourself tour, [Australia, United Kingdom, Europe and Asia], 1990
Blue cotton double-breasted jacket and shorts with Australian flag motif and white sequin body suit

Suzanna Burgess, born UK, 1975
Intimate and Live tour [Australia and London], 1998
['Dancing Queen']
Pink, silver and white sequin, bugle bead and fringe 'showgirl' corset
Co-designed by Kylie Minogue and William Baker

[Encore: 'Confide In Me']
Pistachio satin fringe dress with V-shaped hem and neckline
Co-designed by Kylie Minogue and William Baker

Mark Burnett, born Vietnam, 1971
Intimate and Live tour [Australia and London], 1998
['Cowboy Style']
Blue processed sequin strapless dress with pink beaded appliqué trim and fringed hem

[Encore: 'Better the Devil You Know']
Red lamé corset dress with beaded appliqué and sequin trim

Mushroom 25, Melbourne Cricket Ground, 14 November 1998
Red Japanese polyester tracksuit with hot pink piping and buttons, and silver foil collar

Jimmy Choo, born Malaysia, 1961
Mushroom 25, Melbourne Cricket Ground, 14 November 1998
Red leather high-heel shoes with straps

KylieFever2002 tour [United Kingdom, Europe and Australia]
Act One 'Silvanemesis'. Planet Earth. The Distant Future.
Silver nappa leather lace-up thigh-length boots

Collette Dinnigan, born South Africa, 1965
Moulin Rouge! premiere, Odeon Cinema, Leicester Square,
London, 3 September 2001
Black net dress with black sequins and antique
flesh-coloured lace panels

Domenico Dolce, born Italy, 1958 &
Stefano Gabbana, born Italy, 1962
'Your Disco Needs You' [2001] video from
the album *Light Years*, 2000
Red patent 'mock croc' leather belt with white belt buckle

Madonna concert, Brixton Academy, London, 28 January 2000
Brown suede coat with silver crystal and sequin embroidery

MTV Europe Music Awards, Festhalle, Frankfurt,
Germany, 8 November 2001
White chiffon asymmetrical Grecian dress. Black leather belt
with gold plated logo letters. Chiffon hood. White leather
high-heel shoes with multiple straps and gold ring

'Come Into My World' [2002] video from the album *Fever*, 2001
Pink jersey polo T-shirt with black and white stripe and 'Italia' logo.
Black, white and brown wool herringbone trousers
with Dolce & Gabbana logo around waistband

BRIT Awards, Earl's Court, London, 20 February 2002
White stretch cotton mini corset dress with
flesh-coloured lace-up side panel

'In Your Eyes' [2002] video from the album *Fever*, 2001
Red suede knee-length boots with patent leather trim

KylieFever2002 tour [United Kingdom, Europe and Australia]
Act One 'Silvanemesis'. Planet Earth. The Distant Future.
Crystal mesh bra, miniskirt and choker

Act Two 'Droogie Nights'. England in the Near Future.
White stretch zip-up jumpsuit, black leather customised
belt and black PVC bra. Worn with black patent leather
knee-length boots and silver 'KM' jewellery

Act Three 'The Crying Game'. Hollywood, 1940
Black silk corset dress with black lacing at
sides and antique lace panels

Act Four 'Street Style'. Buffalo, New York, USA. 1982.
Stretch satin shirt with fluorescent trim, navy cotton
drill hipster trousers with braces, white mesh 'Slim Lady'
singlet and fluorescent orange bra. Worn with
customised police hat, fingerless leather gloves, gold
'KM' jewellery and black leather ankle boots

Act Five 'Sex in Venice'. Venice, Italy. Late Eighteenth Century.
Gold stretch satin corset and knickers trimmed with
black lace and ribbon. Black lace wrist ruffs.
Gold loop earrings with diamanté clasp

Act Six 'Cybertronica'. Cyberspace.
An Alternate Timeline. About Now.
White cotton drill combat trousers with fluorescent detail and pink
stretch jersey asymmetrical tanktop with quilted collar detail.
Fluorescent 'KM' bangles and fluorescent pink and white leather
ankle boots.

Encore: 'Voodooinferno'
Black woven mini dress with orange feather trim braid
and loose strips of leather and beading.

Gold hoop earrings with feathers attached and gold
vinyl thigh-high boots with leopard-print lining

Encore
Cream cotton waistcoat and beige needle corduroy
combat trousers with brown leather trim. White
cotton trilby with white grosgrain ribbon band.
Yellow nappa leather 'Banana' stilettos

KylieFever2002 tour, end of tour party, Milan, 11 June 2002
Gold lamé asymmetrical top and miniskirt with matching visor
Leather belt with coins attached and coin arm bands

MTV Europe Music Awards, Sant Jordi Palace,
Barcelona, Spain, 14 November 2002
Pale pink leather buckle hipster trousers and silver
mesh layered singlet top

BRIT Awards, Earl's Court, London, 20 February, 2003
Oyster pink stretch satin dress with flesh-coloured lacing at sides

MTV Europe Music Awards, Ocean Terminal Arena,
Edinburgh, Scotland, 6 November 2003
Green chiffon empire line dress with jewelled trim
and silver leather shoes with jewel trim

'I Believe In You' video from the album *Ultimate Kylie*, 2004
Purple chiffon cut-away dress with crystal mesh straps and waistband

Fee Doran, born UK [for Mrs Jones]
'Can't Get You Out of My Head' video
from the album *Fever*, 2001
White jersey hooded jumpsuit with draped front opening
and extended slits in trousers and sleeves

'In Your Eyes' [2002] video from the album *Fever*, 2001
Two-piece multi-coloured leather ribbon
dress with blanket stitch detail

An Audience With Kylie television special, ITV Network,
London, 22 September 2001
Dyed polyester georgette cape with leather
straps at neck, wrist and ankles

Red jersey strapless jumpsuit with front leg splits
and red leather wrist bands, belt and bowtie

MTV Spring Break, Cancun, Mexico, 13 March 2002
White string vest dress woven through with
multi-coloured leather fringe pieces

John Galliano, born Gibraltar, 1960
'Rhythm of Life' Fashion Charity Gala,
Grosvenor Hotel, London, June 1992
White cotton singlet with paper trim and girdle skirt with chiffon strips

Kylie Showgirl: The Greatest Hits Tour, 2005
[United Kingdom and Europe]
Act One 'Showgirl'. A Deco Revue.
Head dress of blue and white ostrich feathers and star-shaped
Swarovski crystals with blue satin base and ribbon ties.
Blue satin halter-neck corset embroidered with star-shaped
Swarovski crystals and sequins with flesh-coloured inserts at hips.
Blue and white ostrich feather bustle with spray of
star-shaped Swarovski crystals on wire stems

Owen Gaster, born Lebanon, 1970
'Where the Wild Roses Grow' with Nick Cave and The Bad
Seeds, *Top of the Pops*, BBC Television, London, 1995
Green devoré silk, bias-cut slip dress with 'beetle' detail

Jean Paul Gaultier, born France, 1952
Money Can't Buy concert, Carling Apollo Theatre,
Hammersmith, London, 15 November 2003
Breton striped wool cropped sweater

Sandy Gordon, born UK
Royal Variety Performance, Dominion Theatre,
London, 5 December 2000
Red taffeta corsetted Victorian music hall fringe
dress with antique silver lace panels
and silver net
Co-designed with Stevie Stewart

An Audience With Kylie television special,
ITV Network, London, 22 September 2001
Black ribbon tile corset with crystal bugle bead fringe
Co-designed with William Baker and Stevie Stewart

'Can't Get You Out of My Head' video
from the album *Fever*, 2001
Lavender halter-neck dress with polyester satin, ribbon tile trim
Based on Gucci design
Co-designed with Stevie Stewart

'Red Blooded Woman' [2004] video from
the album *Body Language*, 2003
Black dyed sheepskin shrug and black satin waist syncher
Co-designed with William Baker

Top of the Pops, BBC Television, London, 28 November 2003
Transparent PVC waist syncher studded with Swarovski crystals
Co-designed with William Baker

Cosmo Jenks, born UK
An Audience With Kylie television special, ITV Network,
London, 22 September, 2001
Red felt trilby with sequined bow and feather trim
Leopard print faux fur trilby with appliqué trim
Black mesh trilby with red and pink diamantés

Stephen Jones, born UK, 1957
On a Night Like This tour
[United Kingdom, Europe and Australia], 2000
['Broadway']
White mini top hat

[Encore: 'Light Years']
White silk crêpe and blue perspex mini visor

Royal Variety Performance, Dominion Theatre,
London, 5 December 2000
Mini red top hat with net trim and crystal band

An Audience With Kylie television special, ITV Network,
London, 22 September, 2001
Winged head dress with black and oilskin
feathers and black Swarovski crystals

G-A-Y at the London Astoria, 28 February 2004
Black silk top hat with Swarovski crystal band

Lisa King, born Thailand, 1983
'The Museum Dress', 2004
Silk screen-printed dress with fitted bodice and random
fabric swatches and trim. Pink and black tulle underskirt.
Co-designed with Kylie Minogue and Frank Strachan
Realised by Edward Meadham

Nobuhiko Kitamura for Hysteric Glamour, born Japan
Let's Get to It album cover, 1991
Multicoloured, vanity print stretch lycra dress

Karl Lagerfeld, born Germany, 1938
Ivor Novello Awards, Le Meridien Grosvenor House,
London, 22 May 2003
Black and white wool dress. Monogrammed leather
belt featuring chain and pearl attachment

Kylie Showgirl: The Greatest Hits Tour, 2005
Act Five 'Dreams'. A Sound Stage. Hollywod, USA. The Thirties.
Pale pink chiffon fitted dress with Swarovski crystal covered
shoe string straps and V-shaped insert. Trimmed with clusters
of clear glass beads, Swarovski crystals and ostrich feathers
[for Chanel Couture]

Helmut Lang, born Austria, 1956
'Chocolate' [2004] video from the album *Body Language*, 2003
Long red dress with gathered, pleated chiffon detailing
and horse-hair panels in skirt [Couture]

Money Can't Buy concert, Carling Apollo Theatre,
Hammersmith, London, 15 November 2003
Three-tone cotton jersey four-piece dress with metallic
leather side pouch and black cotton jersey arm band

Véronique Leroy, born Belgium, 1965
Lesbian, Gay, Bisexual and Transgender Pride concert,
Clapham Common, London, 6 July 1996
Hot pink chiffon halter-neck dress rouched dress

Impossible Princess, album cover,1998
Blue, black and white nylon and lycra mini dress with
asymmetrical neckline and flared net insert in skirt

Rafael Lopez, born Spain
Royal Variety Performance, Carling Apollo Theatre,
Hammersmith, London, 2 December 2002
Peach cotton jersey mini dress with bronze square sequin panel
[Performance]

Blue silk fringe dress draped from centre front to centre back seam
[Red Carpet]

Julien Macdonald, born UK, 1972
On a Night Like This tour
[United Kingdom, Europe and Australia], 2000
['Loveboat']
Silk embroidered robe with Swarovski crystals

['Physical']
Knitted asymmetrical gold dress with Swarovski crystals

['Butterfly']
Swarovski crystal draped chain bra top [realised by Johnny Rocket]
Gold leather trousers

[Encore: 'Light Years']
Blue and white silk crêpe corset with pleated miniskirt

[Final Encore: 'Spinning Around']
White denim and Swarovski crystal hotpants
worn with jewelled leather belt
Cotton singlet and silk scarf both covered with Swarovski crystals

16th Annual Aria Awards, Superdome,
Homebush Bay, Sydney, 15 October 2002
White silk, long dress with asymmetrical hemline and
low back, trimmed with bands of Swarovski crystals

Smash Hits Poll Winners Party, London Arena,
London, 9 December 2001
Blue denim jeans encrusted with coloured sequins
and stones and Swarovski crystals

BRIT Awards, Earl's Court, London, 20 February 2003
Black silk jersey mini dress with Swarovski
crystal collar and back straps

Stella McCartney, born UK, 1972 [for Chloé]
'Spinning Around' video from the album *Light Years*, 2000
Gold jersey top with gold chain neck and back straps
White cotton drill 'batty rider' shorts

'Come Into My World' [2002] video from the album *Fever*, 2001
Grey suede bag with gold leather piping and double shoulder strap

Ian McMaugh, born Australia, 1954
'Wouldn't Change A Thing' video from the album
Enjoy Yourself, 1989
Cream lycra bra and miniskirt trimmed with strands of artificial pearls

'Disco in Dreams' tour [Japan], 1989
Pink stretch polyester satin top trimmed with sequin
braid and matching hotpants with drop mirror beads

'Better the Devil You Know' video from the
album *Rhythm of Love*, 1990
Silver lamé hotpants

Enjoy Yourself tour,
[Australia, United Kingdom, Europe and Asia], 1990
Black lycra catsuit with silver, blue, gold and red
sequin patches to create 'Mondrian' effect

Alexander McQueen, born UK, 1969
'Spinning Around' video from the album *Light Years*, 2000
Red silk jersey halter-neck top with nylon thread choker
and metal clasp

'Chocolate' [2004] video from the album *Body Language*, 2003
Beige gathered chiffon dress with leather detail

Echo German Music Awards, International Congress Centre,
Berlin, 6 March 2004
Black and flesh-coloured lace corset dress with knitted 'shrug' top

Edward Meadham, born UK, 1979
G-A-Y at the London Astoria, 28 February 2004
Black crinkle silk chiffon and diamanté wraparound skirt

Xen Pardoe Miles
Sydney Gay and Lesbian Mardi Gras Party, Royal Hall
of Industries, Sydney Showgrounds, 5 March 1994
Pink silk corset dress with feather skirt and mirror heart trim

Kylie Minogue, born Australia, 1968
'Did It Again' video [1997] from the album
Impossible Princess, 1998
'Sex Kylie'
Turquoise lycra with black snakeskin print
mini dress with matching waist syncher
Co-designed with William Baker and Stephen Dasilva

Intimate and Live tour [Australia and London], 1998
['Dancing Queen']
Pink, silver and white sequin, bugle bead and fringe 'showgirl' corset
Co-designed with William Baker. Realised by Suzanna Burgess [UK]

[Encore: 'Confide In Me']
Pistachio satin fringe dress with V-shaped hem and neckline
Co-designed with William Baker. Realised by Suzanna Burgess [UK]

'The Museum Dress', 2004
Silk screen-printed dress with fitted bodice and random
fabric swatches and trim. Pink and black tulle underskirt.
Co-designed with Frank Strachan and Lisa King
Realised by Edward Meadham [UK]

Roland Mouret, born France, 1961
'On a Night Like This' video from the album *Light Years*, 2000
Black silk jersey, bias-cut dress with Swarovski
crystal trim and cut-out detail on skirt

'Red Blooded Woman' [2004] video from
the album *Body Language*, 2003
Black and white woven nylon singlet

Louise Olsen, born Australia, 1964, Stephen
Ormandy, born Australia, 1964, and Liane Rossler,
born Australia, 1965 [for Dinosaur Designs]
'Better the Devil You Know' video from the
album *Rhythm of Love*, 1990
Three-stranded yellow resin necklace

Emilio Pucci, born Italy, 1914
Top of the Pops, BBC Television, London, 28 November 2003
Cotton button-up romper suit and perspex platform
shoes studded with Swarovski crystals

Phillip Rhodes, born Australia
Intimate and Live tour [Australia and London], 1998
['Dancing Queen']
Pink ostrich feather and diamanté 'showgirl' tiara

Johnny Rocket, born UK
BRIT Awards, Earl's Court, London, 20 February 2002
'K' tag jewellery

'In Your Eyes' video [2002] from the album *Fever*, 2001
Sterling silver 'Kylie' knuckle-duster ring

KylieFever2002 tour [United Kingdom, Europe and Australia]
Act One 'Silvanemesis'. Planet Earth. The Distant Future.
Silver fibreglass armbands with silver leather fastenings

BRIT Awards, Earl's Court, London, 20 February, 2003
Sterling silver 'JT' heart logo chain and earrings

Martine Sitbon, born Morocco, 1951
46th Annual Grammy Awards, Staples Centre,
Los Angeles, 8 February 2004
Pale pink, silk jersey and net layered dress

Paul Smith, born UK, 1947
Kylie Minogue album cover, 1994
Green silk taffeta two-piece suit
Paul Smith replica

Stevie Stewart, born UK [for Bodymap]
Royal Variety Performance, Dominion Theatre,
London, 5 December 2000
Red taffeta corseted Victorian music hall fringe dress
with antique silver lace panels and silver net
Co-designed with Sandy Gordon

'Can't Get You Out of My Head' video
from the album *Fever*, 2001
Halter-neck mini dress trimmed with layers of folded
lavender coloured ribbon. Based on Gucci design
Co-designed with Sandy Gordon

An Audience With Kylie television special, ITV Network,
London, 22 September 2001
Black ribbon tile corset with crystal bugle bead fringe
Co-designed with William Baker and Sandy Gordon

Money Can't Buy concert, Carling Apollo Theatre,
Hammersmith, London, 15 November 2003
Black stretch high-waisted leggings with black button side detail
White jersey panelled catsuit with white silk waist
syncher, studded with Swarovski crystals

Frank Strachan, born UK, 1979
'The Museum Dress', 2004
Silk screen-printed dress with fitted bodice and random
fabric swatches and trim. Pink and black tulle underskirt.
Co-designed with Kylie Minogue and Lisa King
Realised by Edward Meadham [UK]

Giambattista Valli, born Italy, 1966 [for Emanuel Ungaro]
Laureus Sports Awards, Grimaldi Forum, Monaco, 20 May 2003
Red, ruched silk jersey dress with necktie

MTV Video Music Awards, Radio City Music Hall,
New York, 29 August 2003
White jersey drape dress with crystal-studded star brooch

Vivienne Westwood, born UK, 1941
Money Can't Buy concert, Carling Apollo Theatre,
Hammersmith, London, 15 November 2003
Black suede peep-toe shoes

Hilary Wili, born UK, 1967
G-A-Y at the London Astoria, 17 June 2000
Gold sequin dress with flesh-coloured net bodice covered
in gold sequin appliqué with skirt of long sequin strips

Michael Wilkinson, born Australia
Olympic Games Closing Ceremony, Olympic Stadium,
Sydney, 1 October 2000
Long gold sequin-mesh dress with halter-neck and gold metal trim
Realised by Julie Bryant [Australia]

Paralympics Opening Ceremony, Olympic Stadium,
Sydney, 18 October 2000
Gold PVC trousers and halter-neck corset top with gold plated
chains and studs
Realised by Julie Bryant [Australia]

Scott Wilson, born UK
BRIT Awards, Earl's Court, London, 20 February, 2003
Pink perspex visor and Swarovski crystal cuff

Vintage

Bon Choix
'What Do I Have To Do?' [1991] video from
the album *Rhythm of Love*, 1990
Black, polyester crêpe, vintage dress. Side seams
split to hip with white stripe detail

Designer Unknown
'Spinning Around' video from the album *Light Years*, 2000
Gold lamé hotpants ruched at sides

Saks Fifth Avenue [USA]
'Step Back In Time' video from the album *Rhythm of Love*, 1990
Vintage peach polyester crêpe dress with coin
trim around neckline and matching belt

Frank Usher [UK]
KylieFever2002 tour [United Kingdom, Europe and Australia]
After concert birthday party, Wembley Arena, 27 May 2002
Cream silk floor-length vintage dress with slashed sleeves
and gold trim at waist

Labels

Agent Provocateur [UK]
KylieFever2002 tour [United Kingdom, Europe and Australia]
Act Five 'Sex in Venice'. Venice, Italy. Late Eighteenth Century.
Black polka dot patent leather peep-toe shoes with bows

Chloé [UK]
Smash Hits Poll Winners Party, London, 9 December 2001
White stretch cotton, screen-printed singlet with
Swarovski crystal trim and zip detail

Gina [UK]
Spinning Around [2000] video
from the album *Light Years*, 2000
Gold leather high heel shoes

EXHIBITION CHECKLIST

Olympic Games Closing Ceremony, Olympic Stadium,
Sydney, 1 October 2000
Gold leather T-bar shoes with diamanté trim

Juicy Couture [UK]
Red Blooded Woman [2004] video from
the album *Body Language*, 2003
Blue stretch denim hipster jeans. Customised by Judy Blame [UK]

La Obra [USA]
'Confide In Me' video from the album *Kylie Minogue*, 1994
Camouflage polyester lycra shorts and matching
sleeveless button-up jacket

Lock and Co. Hatters [UK]
KylieFever2002 tour [United Kingdom, Europe and Australia]
Act Two 'Droogie Nights'. England in the Near Future.
Black felt bowler hat

Rigby & Peller, Knightsbridge [UK]
Rhythm of Love tour [Australia and Asia], 1991
Black PVC bodice with criss-cross straps at back

Shellys [UK]
On a Night Like This tour
[United Kingdom, Europe and Australia], 2000
['Butterfly']
Gold leather ankle boots

Viktor and Rolf
'Your Disco Needs You' [2001] video from
the album *Light Years*, 2000
Uncle Sam print cotton pedal pusher trousers

Unknown
'Je Ne Sais Pas Pourquoi' video from the album *Kylie*, 1988
Grey strapless rayon twill dress with sweetheart neckline

'Hand on Your Heart' video from the album *Enjoy Yourself*, 1989
Yellow silk dress with halter neckline and blue appliqué heart trim

Rhythm of Love tour [Australia and Asia], 1991
Black PVC hotpants

'Finer Feelings' [1992] video from the album *Lets Get To It*, 1991
Black rayon velvet dress and bib trimmed with black rooster feathers

'Confide In Me' video from the album *Kylie Minogue*, 1994
Yellow faux fur cropped jacket and fluorescent orange lycra hotpants

'German Bold Italic' video. Single recorded with Towa Tei, 1998
Green silk kimono obi and red resin thongs
Purchased in New York

ARCHIVAL MATERIAL

Royalauto, Official Magazine of the Royal Automobile
Club of Victoria, Australia, April 1988
Kindly lent by Jeff Busby

'The Kylie Bible', *Dazed & Confused*, London, 1994
Kindly lent by Terry Blamey Management

Promotional stickers for the single 'Confide in Me' from
the album *Kylie Minogue*, United Kingdom, 1994
Kindly lent by Terry Blamey Management

Postcard for the album *Kylie Minogue*,
Mushroom Records, Australia, 1994
Kindly lent by Terry Blamey Management

Production schedule for 'Red Blooded Woman'
video shoot, Los Angeles, 2003
Courtesy Darenote Ltd and EMI Records Ltd
Kindly lent by Terry Blamey Management

Program, *Enjoy Yourself* tour, Australia, 1990
Gift of Michael Reason, 1991
Performing Arts Collection
the Arts Centre, Melbourne

Press pass and itinerary, *Enjoy Yourself* tour, Europe, 1990
Kindly lent by Terry Blamey Management

Program, *Intimate and Live* tour, 1998
Gift of Terry Blamey Management, 2004
Performing Arts Collection
the Arts Centre, Melbourne

'Access All Areas' pass and itinerary
Intimate and Live tour, Australia, 1998
Kindly lent by Terry Blamey Management

Program, *On a Night Like This* tour, 2001
Kindly lent by Darenote Ltd

'Access All Areas' pass, *On a Night Like This* tour, Australia, 2001
Gift of William Baker, 2006
Performing Arts Collection
the Arts Centre, Melbourne

Itinerary, *KylieFever2002* tour, Australia
Gift of Terry Blamey Management, 2004
Performing Arts Collection
the Arts Centre, Melbourne

Program and metallic envelope, *KylieFever2002* tour
Kindly lent by Darenote Ltd

'VIP' pass, 'Guest' pass and ticket,
KylieFever2002 tour, United Kingdom
Kindly lent by Terry Blamey Management

Program, *Kylie Showgirl: The Greatest Hits Tour*, 2005
Gift of Terry Blamey Management, 2005
Performing Arts Collection
the Arts Centre, Melbourne

'VIP' pass, wristband and tickets
Kylie Showgirl: The Greatest Hits Tour, 2005
Kindly lent by Terry Blamey Management

AWARDS

All awards kindly lent by Kylie Minogue

Silver Logie award for 'Most Popular Australian Actress',
TV Week Logie Awards, Australia, 1986

Platinum record for the single 'Locomotion',
Mushroom Records and Festival Records, Australia, 1987

'Highest Selling Single' award for 'Locomotion',
Australian Record Industry Awards, 1987

Gold Logie award for 'Most Popular Personality on
Australian Television', *TV Week* Logie Awards, Australia, 1987

'Best Female Solo' award, *Smash Hits* Readers Poll,
United Kingdom, 1988

Silver sales award for 'I Should Be So Lucky', British
Phonographic Industry, United Kingdom, 1988

Multi-platinum record for the album *Kylie*, British
Phonographic Industry, United Kingdom, 1988

'Outstanding Achievement' award,
Australian Record Industry Awards, 1989

Platinum sales award for the single 'Confide in Me',
Mushroom Records, Australia, 1994

Gold single for 'Where the Wild Roses Grow',
Liberation Records, Australia, 1995

Platinum sales award for the album
Impossible Princess, Mushroom Records,
Australia, 1998

'Best Pop Release' award for the single
'Spinning Around', ARIA Music Awards, Australia, 2000

Quadruple platinum sales award for the album
Light Years, Festival Mushroom Records, Australia, 2001

Award for the *On a Night Like This* tour,
Sydney Entertainment Centre, Australia, 2001

Multi-platinum award for the single, 'Can't Get You Out of My
Head', British Phonographic Industry, United Kingdom, 2001

'Services to Mankind' award, *GQ Men Of The Year*,
United Kingdom, 2001

'Best Female Artist' award, ARIA Music Awards, Australia, 2001

Triple platinum award for the album *Fever*, EMI, Norway, 2001

'Best Chart Act' award for the single 'Can't Get You Out
of My Head', DanceStar, United Kingdom, 2002

'Top Tour' award for *KylieFever2002*,
Top of the Pops Awards, United Kingdom, 2002

'Best Selling Australian Recording Artist' award,
World Music Awards, Monte Carlo, Monaco, 2002

'Best Choreography in a Video' award for 'Can't Get You
Out of My Head', MTV Video Music Awards, USA, 2002

'Best Pop Act' award, MTV Europe Awards, 2002

'Best International Female Solo Artist' award, British
Record Industry Trust, United Kingdom, 2002

'Best International Album' award for *Fever*, British
Record Industry Trust, United Kingdom, 2002

Grammy Award for 'Best Dance Recording' for the
single 'Come into My World', National Academy
of Recording Arts & Sciences, USA, 2003

COSTUME DESIGNS

All designs kindly lent by Darenote Ltd

Dolce & Gabbana [Italy] 2002
KylieFever2002 tour
Act One 'Silvanemesis'. Planet Earth. The Distant Future.
Indian ink, paint, felt-tip pen and ballpoint pen on colour photocopy

Act Two 'Droogie Nights'. England in the Near Future.
Indian ink, water colour paints and felt-tip pen on paper.

Act Four 'Street Style'. Buffalo, New York, USA, 1982
Felt-tip pen on paper

Act Five 'Sex in Venice'. Venice, Italy. Late Eighteenth Century
Indian ink, water colour paint and felt-tip pen on paper

Act Six 'Cybertronica'. Cyberspace.
An Alternate Timeline. About Now
Indian ink, water colour paint, felt-tip pen and pencil on paper

Encore: 'Voodooinferno'
Indian ink, water colour paint, felt-tip pen and pencil on paper

Encore
Colour photocopy

Edward Griffiths [UK] 2002
KylieFever2002 tour
Prelude: Kyborg
Pencil and paint on paper

Fee Doran for Mrs Jones [UK] 2001
'Can't Get You Out of My Head', *Fever*, 2001
Pencil on paper

OBJECTS

Unknown
'Did It Again' video [1997] from the album
Impossible Princess, 1998
'Indie Kylie' black perforated plastic prop
name board with white plastic letters
Gift of Kylie Minogue, 2004
Performing Arts Collection
the Arts Centre, Melbourne

PHOTOGRAPHS

Mark Abrahams, born USA, 1957
Photo shoot
Cover and feature published in *Elle* [UK], May 2004
Los Angeles
Type C print
Courtesy Mark Abrahams

**Mert Alas, born Turkey, 1971 and
Marcus Piggott, born UK, 1971**
Photo shoot
Cover and feature published in *Pop*, Spring/Summer 2002
London
Type C print
Courtesy Darenote Ltd

Promotional shoot for the album *Body Language*, August 2003
St Tropez, France
Type C prints
Courtesy Darenote Ltd and EMI Records Ltd

Bill Bachman, born USA, 1952; arrived Australia, 1973
Photo shoot for the video 'Hand on Your Heart'
from the album, *Enjoy Yourself*, 1989
Melbourne
Type C print
Courtesy KDB Pty Ltd and PAL Productions Ltd

Pierre Bailly, born France, 1973
Photo shoot
'You Were Never Lovelier' feature published
in *Pop 7* [UK], Autumn/Winter 2003
Coco Chanel's Apartment, 31 Rue Cambon, Paris
Type C prints
Courtesy Darenote Ltd
Kindly lent by Pierre Bailly

William Baker, born UK, 1973
Photo shoot for *Kylie Showgirl: Homecoming Tour*, 2006
Lido, Paris
Type C prints
Courtesy Darenote Ltd and William Baker

Photo shoot for Kylie's 2007 calendar, 2006
London
Type C print
Courtesy Darenote Ltd and William Baker

David LaChappelle, born USA, 1969
Photo shoot
Cover and feature published in *Flaunt* [USA], Spring 2002
Santa Monica Pier, Los Angeles
Type C print
Kindly lent by David LaChappelle

Photo shoot
Cover and feature published in *Flaunt* [USA], Spring 2002
Los Angeles
Type C print
Kindly lent by David LaChappelle

James Dimmock, born UK, 1972
Photo shoot
Cover and feature published in GQ [UK], October 2001
London
Type C print
Courtesy James Dimmock

Simon Emmett, born UK, 1969
Promotional shoot for *Intimate and Live* tour, 1998
London
Type C print
Courtesy Darenote Ltd and Simon Emmett

Photo shoot
Cover and feature published in GQ [UK], January 2005
London
Type C prints
Courtesy Darenote Ltd and Simon Emmett

Robert Erdmann, born USA
Photo shoot for the single 'What Do I Have to Do?'
[1991] from the album, *Rhythm of Love*, 1990
London
Type C print
Courtesy Darenote Ltd and PAL Productions Ltd

Simon Fowler, born Australia, 1954
Photo shoot for the album *Enjoy Yourself*, 1989
London
Type C print
Courtesy Darenote Ltd and PAL Productions Ltd

Katerina Jebb, born UK, 1962
Photo shoot for the single 'Finer Feelings' [1992]
from the album *Let's Get To It*, 1991

Photo shoot, 1993
Romden Hall House, Kent, United Kingdom
Type C print
Courtesy Darenote Ltd

Paris
Type C print
Courtesy Darenote Ltd and PAL Productions Ltd

Photo shoot, one in a series inspired by the Playboy Bunny, 1994
Sydney
Gelatin silver print
Kindly lent by Kylie Minogue

Photo shoot for limited edition book
published by deConstruction, 1994
London
Type C print
Courtesy Darenote Ltd and deConstruction/BMG Ltd

Promotional shoot for deConstruction, 1994
Katherine Hamnett, Sloane Street, London
Type C print
Courtesy Darenote Ltd and deConstruction/BMG Ltd

Photo shoot, 1994
Romden Hall House, Kent, United Kingdom
Type C print
Courtesy Darenote Ltd

Photo shoot
Published in 'The Elevator Issue', *i-D* [UK], No. 191, October 1999
London
Type C print
Courtesy Darenote Ltd

Photo shoot for the single 'Breathe' from the
album *Impossible Princess*, 1998
London
Type C print
Courtesy Darenote Ltd and deConstruction/BMG Ltd

Promotional shoot for the album *Body Language*, 2003
Paris
Type C print
Courtesy Darenote Ltd and EMI Records Ltd

Promotional shoot for the album *Body Language*, 2003
Ritz Hotel, Paris
Type C print
Courtesy Darenote Ltd and EMI Records Ltd

Lee Jenkins, born UK
Photo shoot
Published in *The Face* [UK], January 2002
London
Type C print
Courtesy Darenote Ltd

Karl Lagerfeld, born Germany, 1938
Photo shoot for 'The Divine Miss M', one in a series commissioned
by and published in *Vogue Australia*, December 2003
Paris
Inkjet print
Courtesy Darenote Ltd and Karl Lagerfeld
Kindly lent by Kylie Minogue

Lawrence Lawry, born UK, 1956
Photo shoot for the single 'Got To Be Certain'
from the album *Kylie*, 1988
HDG Studios, London
Type C print
Courtesy Darenote Ltd and PAL Productions Ltd

Andrew Macpherson, born UK
Photo shoot
Cover and feature published in *The Face* [UK], No. 37, October 1991
London
Type C print
Courtesy Darenote Ltd and Andrew Macpherson

Ali Mahdavi, born Iran, 1974
Photo shoot
Cover and feature published in *WestEast Magazine*, 2002
London
Type C print
Courtesy Darenote Ltd and Ali Mahdavi

Grant Matthews, born Australia, 1953
Photo shoot
Cover and feature published in *Follow Me* [Australia], December 1990
Sydney
Inkjet print
Courtesy KDB Pty Ltd and Grant Matthews

George Miller, born UK, 1948
Photo shoot for the video 'Locomotion' from the album *Kylie*, 1987
Melbourne
Type C print
Courtesy KDB Pty Ltd and PAL Productions

Markus Morianz, born Austria, 1965
Photo shoot for the album *Rhythm of Love*, 1990
Bonaventuru Tower, Los Angeles
Type C print
Courtesy Darenote Ltd and PAL Productions Ltd

Photo shoot for the album *Rhythm of Love*, 1990
El Mirage Dry Lake, Mojave Desert, USA
Type C print
Courtesy Darenote Ltd and PAL Productions Ltd

Xevi Muntane, born Spain, 1977
Promotional shoot for the *KylieFever2002* tour, 2001
London
Type C print
Courtesy Darenote Ltd

Photo shoot
'Pin-Up' cover and feature published in *V Man* [USA], 2004
New York
Type C photograph
Courtesy Darenote Ltd

Promotional shoot for the album, *Ultimate Kylie*, 2004
London
Type C print
Courtesy Darenote Ltd and EMI Records Ltd

Photo shoot for the single 'I Believe in You'
from the album, *Ultimate Kylie*, 2004
London
Type C photograph
Courtesy Darenote Ltd and EMI Records Ltd

PAL Productions Ltd
Photo shoot for the video 'I Should Be So Lucky'
from the album *Kylie*, 1987
Melbourne
Type C print
Courtesy KDB Ltd and PAL Productions

Vincent Peters, born Germany, 1969
Photo shoot for the album *Light Years*, 2000
Ibiza Island, Spain
Type C print
Courtesy Darenote Ltd and EMI Records Ltd

Photo shoot for the album *Fever*, 2001
London
Type C prints
Courtesy Darenote Ltd and EMI Records Ltd

Steve Rapport, born UK, 1956
Photo shoot, 1990
Taken on the set of the video for the single 'What Do I Have to Do?'
London
Type C print
Courtesy Darenote Ltd and PAL Productions Ltd

Bert Stern, born USA, 1930 and
Baz Luhrmann, born Australia, 1962
Photo shoot for 'Star' which featured Kylie in
a picture spread as 'Judy Lamour'
Published in *Vogue Australia*, January 1994
Universal Studios, Los Angeles
Gelatin silver prints
Courtesy Bert Stern and Baz Luhrmann
Kindly lent by Kylie Minogue

Juergen Teller, born Germany, 1964
Photo shoot for the album *Let's Get To It*, 1991
London
Gelatin silver prints
Courtesy PAL Productions Ltd and Juergen Teller
Kindly lent by Kylie Minogue

Tesh, born UK, 1972
Photo shoot
Published in *i-D* [UK], November 2003
London
Type C print
Courtesy Darenote Ltd

Promotional shoot for the single 'Chocolate'
from the album *Body Language*, 2004
London
Type C print
Courtesy Darenote Ltd and EMI Records Ltd

Ellen von Unwerth, born Austria, 1954
Photo shoot for the single 'Shocked' [1991]
from the album *Rhythm of Love*, 1990
Paris
Type C print
Courtesy Darenote Ltd, PAL Productions and Ellen von Unwerth

Photo shoot for the single 'Word is Out' from
the album *Let's Get To It*, 1991
Paris
Type C print
Courtesy Darenote Ltd, PAL Productions and Ellen von Unwerth

Uli Weber, born Germany, 1964; arrived UK, 1986
Photo shoot
Cover and feature first published in 'This Week',
Daily Express, 24 August 1994
London
Type C print

Photo shoot
Cover and feature first published in *The Sunday Times* Magazine,
26 June 1994
London
Type C print
Courtesy Darenote Ltd and Uli Weber

NOTES

KYLIE'S SHOW SHOES

The Kylie Minogue Collection features over 30 pairs of shoes
by some of the world's leading designers, including Agent
Provocateur, Azzedine Alaïa, Manolo Blahnik, Jimmy Choo,
Dolce & Gabbana, Emilio Pucci and Vivienne Westwood.

Unfortunately, we were not always able to photograph the shoes
together with the outfit Kylie wore with them. Where this has
occurred in the catalogue, and the shoes are regarded as integral
to Kylie's overall look, the note [not pictured] has been inserted.

VIDEO: BEHIND THE SCENES

Kylie rediscovered a suite of images which are
featured in the collage on page 22.
Clockwise from top lefthand corner: 'Did It Again', London 1997;
'Can't Get You Out of My Head', London 2001; 'Slow', Barcelona,
2003. Kylie with director Baillie Walsh [left] and choreographer
Michael Rooney [right]; 'Got To Be Certain', Melbourne, 1988;
'Locomotion', Melbourne, 1987; 'Locomotion', Melbourne, 1987.

p.23 'Did it Again' video [1997] from the album
Impossible Princess, 1998
'Indie Kylie' red suede mules with fringe
Designed by Manolo Blahnik [UK]

THE TOURS

Disco in Dreams, 1989, 2–8 October, Japan

Hitman Roadshow, 1989, 12–18 October,
plus seven other dates, UK

Enjoy Yourself, 1990, 3–9 February, Australia,
17 April – 17 May, UK and Europe

Rhythm of Love, 1991
10–23 February, Australia, to 10 March, Asia

Let's Get To It, 1991
25 October – 8 November, UK

Intimate and Live, 1998
2 June – 4 July, Australia, 29–31 July, London

On a Night Like This, 2001
3–20 March, UK, 23–28 March, Europe, 14 April – 12 May, Australia

KylieFever2002
26 April – 27 May, UK, 30 May – 18 June, Europe
2–15 August, Australia

Kylie Showgirl: The Greatest Hits Tour, 2005
19 March – 7 May, UK and Europe

Kylie Showgirl: Homecoming Tour
From December 2006, Australia and UK

Costumes in the catalogue relating to *Intimate and
Live* and *On a Night Like This* have been identified by
shorthand names which refer either to show theme
[eg:'Broadway'] or to song title [eg:'Dancing Queen'].

CREDITS

PHOTOGRAPHY

Cover & Preface
p.13 Xevi Muntane © Darenote Ltd 2004

The Music & Videos
p.19 Ken McKay
p.21 Natalie Stevenson
p.24 'I Should Be So Lucky' video. Courtesy of PAL Productions Ltd
pp.25 & 26 Bill Bachman
p.27 'Wouldn't Change a Thing' video.
Courtesy of PAL Productions Ltd
p.28 Markus Morianz
p.29 'Better the Devil You Know' video. Courtesy of PAL Productions Ltd
p.30 Ron Wolfson
p.31 'What Do I Have to Do?' video. Courtesy of PAL Productions Ltd
p.32 Juergen Teller. Courtesy of PAL Productions Ltd
p.33 Katerina Jebb
pp.34 & 35 Steve Rapport
p.36 Rankin. Courtesy of deConstruction/BMG Ltd
p.37 © 1997 Stephane Sednaoui. All Rights Reserved.
Courtesy of deConstruction/BMG Ltd
pp.38 & 39 'Did It Again' video. Courtesy of deConstruction/BMG Ltd
p.40 © 1997 Stephane Sednaoui. All Rights Reserved.
'German Bold Italic' video. Towa Tei featuring Kylie Minogue.
Courtesy of Warner Music
pp.41, 42 & 44 Paulo Sutch
p.45 Xevi Muntane
p.46 & 48 'Can't Get You Out of My Head' video.
Photograph courtesy Parlophone Records and EMI Records Ltd
p.49 Ken McKay
p.50 Paulo Sutch. Courtesy Parlophone Records and EMI Records Ltd
pp.52 & 53 Ken McKay
p.54 Leanne Woolrich
p.55 Ken McKay

The Tours
p.57 Jasin Boland
p.59 Willam Baker [left], Jasin Boland [right]
pp.60, 61, 62 & 63 Unknown
p.64 Unknown [left]. i-D March 1991 no.90 'The Love Life' issue.
Photography Robert Erdmann. Courtesy i-D [right]
pp.66, 68 & 69 Campbell Knott
p.70 Unknown
p.72 Jasin Boland [left], Unknown [right]
p.74 William Baker
pp.75, 76 & 77 Jasin Boland
p.78 Jasin Boland [left], William Baker [right]
pp.80, 82 & 83 Ken McKay
p.84 Unknown
p.86 Ken McKay, Salvo Nicosia
pp.88 Ken McKay
p.89 Ken McKay [left], William Baker [middle], Ken McKay [right]
pp.90, 92 & 94 Ken McKay

The Performances
p.99 Jason Reed © Reuters/Picture Media
p.100 Richard Young © REX FEATURES/Austral
p.101 Unknown
p.102 Edward Hirst © REX FEATURES/Austral
pp.103 Unknown
p.104 © 1997 Stephane Sednaoui. All Rights Reserved.
Courtesy of deConstruction/BMG Ltd
p.106 Andre Csillag © REX FEATURES/Austral
p.107 Martin Philbey. Courtesy of the Mushroom Group
p.108 Jeff Darmanin © NewsPix
p.109 Jamie Squire © Getty Images
p.110 William Baker
p.111 Nikos Vinieratos © REX FEATURES/Austral
p.112 Dave Hogan © Getty Images
p.114 Sean Fitzpatrick
p.116 Canio Romaniello

p.118 © NewsPix
p.119 Scott Gries © Getty Images
p.120 Dave Bennett © Getty Images
p.121 Jon Furniss © Getty Images
p.122 Dave Bennett © Getty Images
p.124 Courtesy BBC Television
pp.126 to 129 Ken McKay

The Red Carpet
p.134 Unknown
p.135 Tony Kyriacou © REX FEATURES/Austral
p.136 Can Nguyen © London Features/Scope
p.137 Richard Young © REX FEATURES/Austral
p.138 Ian Jennings © London Features/Scope
p.139 MTV Studios/ZUMA Press/Austral
p.140 David Fisher © London Features/Scope
p.142 © Rota/REX FEATURES/Austral
p.143 © REX FEATURES/Austral
p.144 Dave Bennett © Getty Images
p.145 Dennis Van Tine © London Features/Scope
p.146 David Fisher © London Features/Scope
p.147 Frederick M. Brown © Getty Images
p.148 Stefan Schnoor © REX FEATURES/Austral

COSTUME DESIGNS

pp.47 & 50 Fee Doran for Mrs Jones. Courtesy Darenote Ltd & EMI Records Ltd
pp.80, 82, 86 & 116 Dolce & Gabbana. Courtesy Darenote Ltd
pp.92 John Galliano. Courtesy Kylie Minogue and Darenote Ltd
pp.113 & 114 Fee Doran for Mrs Jones. Courtesy Darenote Ltd

CONTRIBUTORS

William Baker

William Baker read Theology at Kings College, University of London, and worked at Vivienne Westwood, before joining Kylie as her stylist and creative director in 1994. A pop aficionado, William is Kylie's major collaborator, working on an increasingly diverse range of projects, including stage and costume design, short films, video direction and writing. He has introduced groundbreaking collaborations which have included the award-winning *KylieFever2002* tour and 2003's *21* produced by Ballet Rambert. He wrote *la la la* with Kylie, published in 2002. William has worked with other artists from time to time including Garbage, Tricky, Björk and Jamiroquai.

Janine Barrand

Janine Barrand is the Manager of Collections & Research at the Arts Centre, Melbourne. She has worked in the performing arts and museums for over 20 years and has a special interest in popular music and contemporary culture. In 1999 Janine was awarded a Churchill Fellowship to study performing arts museums and collections around the world.

Barry Humphries

Barry Humphries is an actor, writer and artist. In 1956 he created the character of Mrs Everage, a Melbourne housewife who became the hugely popular Dame Edna. Since then, his one-man shows have been seen around the world. In 1999 he was awarded a special Tony Award for the Broadway production of *Dame Edna – The Royal Tour.* He is currently performing his latest one-man show, *Dame Edna and friends: Back with a vengeance* in Australia.

Tony Hung

Tony Hung (*Adjective Noun*) is a freelance art director/graphic designer based in London. Since graduating from Manchester Polytechnic in 1996, Tony has directed, designed and consulted on a large variety of projects, numerous music album campaigns and won awards for both his sleeve and book designs. Clients include Columbia, EMI, Island, Mo Wax and Regal Recordings. After designing Kylie's *Fever* album campaign in 2001, Tony has become a member of Kylie's creative team.

Baz Luhrmann

A diverse and creative talent, writer/producer/director Baz Luhrmann is the co-founder of Bazmark Inq., which produces films, opera, theatre, music, multi-media and events worldwide. Known for his artistic integrity and inventive works that tap into the popular imagination, his recent works include *Moulin Rouge!*, Puccini's *La Boheme* on Broadway and the worldwide TV/cinema campaign for Chanel No 5 starring Nicole Kidman. He is currently in pre-production on his next feature film, a sweeping, romantic epic set in the north-west of Australia in the 1930s.

Frank Strachan

Frank Strachan graduated from Central Saint Martins in 2001, with an award-winning menswear collection. Until May 2005, Frank worked with Kylie's creative team on both her personal and performance wardrobes. As a pop obsessive, he is a human database when it comes to the history of Kylie's costumes. Frank's established styling career currently sees him working with several high profile artists, including Jamelia, Girls Aloud, and the Pet Shop Boys.

SELECT BIBLIOGRAPHY

Publications

Baker, W. & Minogue, K. (2002), *Kylie la la la*,
Hodder & Stoughton, Great Britain.

Camp, C. (1990), *Kylie Minogue: The official 1991 annual*,
World International Publishing Ltd, United Kingdom.

Darenote Ltd (1999), *Kylie: evidence*,
Booth-Clibborn Editions, London.

Stone, S. (1990), *Kylie Minogue: The superstar
next door*, Omnibus Press, London.

Watt, A. (1989), *Kylie On the Go*, Dennis Oneshots Ltd, London.

Watt, A. (1989), *Kylie Stardust*, Quadrant Publishing, Surrey.

Watt, A. (1987), *Kylie Minogue*, Australian Consolidated
Press & Greenhouse Publications, Australia.

Web sites

limbo, www.kylie.co.uk

The Official Kylie Web site, www.kylie.com

ACKNOWLEDGEMENTS

The Arts Centre, Melbourne would like to express
thanks to Kylie Minogue, whose performance career
and wonderful costumes inspired *Kylie – The Exhibition*
and catalogue. We would also like to acknowledge
Ron and Carol Minogue for their valued support.

The London-based team is acknowledged, with thanks
in particular to William Baker and Frank Strachan for so
generously sharing their creativity and knowledge with us.
Thank you to Terry Blamey, Allison MacGregor, Claire Pardew
and Leanne Woolrich for their ongoing assistance. Thanks
also to Tony Hung for his contribution to graphic design.

Thank you to all the designers whose work appears in this catalogue,
in particular those who provided quotations: Manolo Blahnik,
Mark Burnett, Collette Dinnigan, Dolce & Gabbana,
Fee Doran, John Galliano, Karl Lagerfeld, Julien Macdonald,
Steven Phillips, Laudomia Pucci and Giambattista Valli.

We thank the photographers who have participated in the exhibition:
Mark Abrahams, Mert Alas, Bill Bachman, William Baker,
Pierre Bailly, James Dimmock, Simon Emmett, Simon Fowler,
David LaChapelle, Lawrence Lawry, Katerina Jebb, Andrew
Macpherson, Ali Mahdavi, Grant Matthews, George Miller, Markus
Morianz, Xevi Muntane, Vincent Peters, Marcus Piggott, Steve
Rapport, Juergen Teller, Tesh, Ellen von Unwerth and Uli Weber.

Thanks also to the many agents and studio managers who assisted
us: Katy Baggott [Deliverance Studio], Fred Bladou, Nick Bryning,
Kate Congreve [ESP], Matthew S. Currie [David LaChapelle
Studio], Natalie Doran [D & V Management], Bianca Escobar
[Tagadaboomboom, Inc.], Ulrike Holler, Patricia McMahon,
Fabiane Mandarino, Terri Manduca, Candice Marks [Art
Partners], Wes Olsen [Macfly], and Sue Southam [Mondo Film].

Many others contributed to *Kylie – The Exhibition*. We acknowledge
BBC Television, Jeff Busby, deConstruction/BMG Ltd, EMI Records Ltd,
Festival Mushroom Records, Anna Higgins, Barry Humphries, Baz
Luhrmann, Amanda Luhrmann, Geoff Harman, *i-D Magazine*,
Mannequin Revolution, Melissa LeGear Management, Ian 'Molly'
Meldrum, Helen Nolan, Jelka Music and Warner Vision Australia.

Special thanks to the Melbourne team who realised the original
exhibition and Australian and UK tour: Zera Haisma for
her exhibition design, Erika Budiman for graphic design and
Fiona Bennie and Rob Gebert for project management. We thank
Jeremy Dillon and Narelle Wilson for costume photography,
Catherine Shannon for cataloguing, Shona Brethouwer and
Elyse White for collection management, Helen Laffin and
Kathryn Kiely for tour registration, Margaret Marshall and
Narelle Symes for research and proof reading, Margaret Trudgeon
for editing, Julia Peddie for finished art, Paul Chierego and
Theo Strasser for technical coordination, Irene Villas for
public programs and Ricky Bryan, Kerry Noonan and Jeremy
Vincent for marketing, publicity and corporate relations.

We also thank the UK venues for so enthusiastically embracing
the international tour. We acknowledge our initial contacts at
each of them: Victoria Broackes and Geoffrey Marsh [V&A's
Theatre Museum]; Tim Wilcox [Manchester Art Gallery];
Mark O'Neil [Kelvingrove Art Gallery and Museum]. Thank
you to Mary Butler [V&A Publications] and the Arts Centre's
UK *Kylie –The Exhibition* representative, Tim McKeough

Finally, special thanks to the exhibition's assistant
curator and my collaborator Margot Anderson for her
professionalism, knowledge and dedication.

Janine Barrand
Curator, *Kylie –The Exhibition*